MENTAL HEALTH IN SCHOOLS

MENTAL HEALTH IN SCHOOLS

A Guide to Pastoral and Curriculum Provision

Mark Prever

P·CP

Paul Chapman
Publishing

British Association for
Counselling and Psychotherapy

© British Association for Counselling and Psychotherapy 2006

First published 2006

Apart from any fair dealing for the purposes of research or
private study, or criticism or review, as permitted under the
Copyright, Designs and Patents Act, 1988, this publication
may be reproduced, stored or transmitted in any form, or by
any means, only with the prior permission in writing of the
publishers, or in the case of reprographic reproduction, in
accordance with the terms of licences issued by the Copyright
Licensing Agency. Enquiries concerning reproduction outside
those terms should be sent to the publishers.

 Paul Chapman Publishing
P·C·P A SAGE Publications Company
1 Oliver's Yard
55 City Road
London EC1Y 1SP

SAGE Publications Inc
2455 Teller Road
Thousand Oaks, California 91320

SAGE Publications India Pvt Ltd
B-42, Panchsheel Enclave
Post Box 4109
New Delhi 110 017

Library of Congress Control Number: 2006928799

A catalogue record for this book is available from the British Library

ISBN-10 1-4129-2330-1   ISBN-13 978-1-4129-2330-9
ISBN-10 1-4129-2331-X   ISBN-13 978-1-4129-2331-6 (pbk)

Typeset by Pantek Arts Ltd, Maidstone, Kent
Printed in Great Britain by Cromwell Press Ltd, Trowbridge, Wiltshire
Printed on paper from sustainable resources

ᴄONTENTS

This book is dedicated to my daughter Miriam
and all young people

ACKNOWLEDGEMENTS

I would like to recognise the importance of all the people I have worked with in numerous settings over the last 30 years or so and whose influence has been real and lasting. In particular, I wish to acknowledge all the children and young people who have worked with me and who have shared many of their hopes, fears, sadness, loss and distress. It really is quite special when young people let you into their life, trusting you with their thoughts and deepest feelings – things that are potentially so hidden and private.

Many thanks to the British Association for Counselling and Psychotherapy for commissioning me to write this book and, in particular, to Lewis Edwards, Marketing and Communications Manager, for keeping me on task and strictly to deadlines.

I also wish to thank all those professionals who have influenced me throughout my career; in particular, Carmel Mullen-Hartley at the Open Door Youth Counselling Service in Birmingham.

I am grateful to my family for their support through difficult times and particularly to my partner Ruth.

Finally, and certainly not least, is my daughter Miriam, who remains special to me in so many ways. Miriam has highlighted the importance of good parenting, security and love in young people's development and in their emotional health and well-being.

ABOUT THE AUTHOR

Mark Prever was born in Hackney, East London, in 1953 and has been involved in education for over 30 years. He is an experienced teacher but has substantial experience also of youth and community work and social work with young people at risk. For many years he has held formal pastoral roles, including Head of Year and Personal Social and Health Education Co-ordinator in a range of secondary schools across Birmingham.

Over the last 16 years, Mark has developed a substantial interest in counselling and is currently Counselling Development Officer at the Open Door Youth Counselling Service in Birmingham where he has previously held the roles of clinical supervisor and Chair of the Agency.

Up until recently, Mark was the manager of a school-based Student Support Centre for young people with social, emotional and behavioural problems as well as holding responsibility for child protection at the school. His current role at the school is Student Development Leader.

Mark has also held the role of Chair of Counselling Children and Young People (CCYP), a division of the British Association for Counselling and Psychotherapy. He maintains a particular interest in counselling and therapeutic work with young people, mental health and emotional literacy in educational settings, and is a trainer and writer in these fields. He has written for a range of journals on related matters and has contributed to radio and the production of TV programmes.

Mark lives in Worcestershire and has a daughter aged 11.

PREFACE

Why write this book?

In writing this book, I have more than a desire to disseminate information about mental health in the context of schooling. I want it to be a useful resource, but I am aware also of a campaigning edge. The book is designed to raise the issues and possibilities of a comprehensive approach to mental health in schools. A concern for the mental health needs of young people, and the school's awareness of these, remains largely hidden. Schools are trying their hardest, often with success, to support young people in difficulty, and many hours are spent with parents and pupils trying to address problems. However, many professionals working in schools will recognise that they feel helpless and deskilled when confronted with young people who are self-harming, socially isolated and withdrawn, or behaving in a way that causes distress at home and school. These outward expressions of sadness, unhappiness or difficulty ultimately affect the learning and well-being of other pupils with whom they come into contact.

I believe that unless education places mental health and well-being at the forefront of planning, schools will remain purely reactive institutions with a 'fire-fighting' model of pastoral care. What is advocated here is a more proactive approach, where problems are anticipated and pre-empted, and where prevention and early intervention are keenly held concepts that influence policy and planning. This book seeks to raise awareness of mental health in schools and challenge schools with a new way of thinking.

Who is it for?

This book is for all adults who work in schools and who come into contact with young people in distress or difficulty. This includes teachers with a pastoral role, whether as form tutor or at the level of middle management. However, I would be pleased if it also appealed to all classroom teachers and assistants and those with newly created pastoral roles as a result of workforce reform. Clearly, these pages will be of use to other staff working in schools, such as learning mentors, special needs teachers and the school special educational needs coordinator. In addition, I hope that the book is read and discussed by school head teachers, other members of the senior leadership team and governors, in particular those with the influence to effect change.

The book is also relevant to the many other professionals working in schools, such as behaviour support, education social workers, educational psychologists and Connexions workers.

In fact, I hope this book will be of interest to anyone who sees schooling as more than an opportunity to pass on knowledge and help pupils achieve in the formal sense, important as these goals may be. It is for all professionals who wish to highlight the importance of promoting the mental health and emotional well-being of young people in our schools.

Importantly, this book is also about working with parents, family and friends whose lives are entwined with the child in distress – or become so. My aim is that the content and ideas explored in the book will open up purposeful and sensitive communication with families, and facilitate the kind of dialogue and sense of working together in partnership that is so necessary for quality support, intelligent home–school contracts and – hopefully – successful outcomes.

How should the book be used?

I want this to be an intensely practical book, written with a passion born out of many years of experience. As indicated above, I also hope that the book will challenge and offer new perspectives on the practice of pastoral care.

The book should be read in full because it is important that the arguments presented are understood. The book can later be returned to for reference and discussion. I would be delighted if the book were used for training and professional development. For this reason, I have included a number of 'reflection boxes' throughout the text at appropriate points. These can be used for self-reflection or in discussion with others. Where a page is headed 'photocopiable', please feel free to reproduce it for work with colleagues. Where material has been designed for pupils to work with, you may make multiple copies for classroom use. In addition, the text is interspersed with a number of 'key points ✐' that attempt to capture the essence of the following pages.

CHAPTER 1

Introduction

This chapter will show that:

Young people in difficulty may have underlying mental health issues. Schools need to look beyond the behaviour to understand what might be going on for that young person. Narrow behavioural approaches are sometimes limited and may make matters worse.

Perhaps the best place to begin is with the following case studies, which introduce us to some of the main issues to be explored throughout this book. These young people do not of course exist, but they represent an amalgam of some of the young people I have known during the last 30 years. While reading, you may recognise elements of some of the pupils you already work with. If I have learnt anything in my years' working with young people, it is the complexity of their lives, the stresses they face, the loss they experience, the violence they encounter. Sometimes I ask myself: how would I cope in their situation? Do I really understand? Can I even begin to feel what they are feeling now?

Carl

Carl is a Year 8 pupil, small for his age. His junior school transfer information shows that he has had problems with his behaviour since Year 4 when his mother and father's relationship reached an all-time low and domestic violence became a feature of the relationship – violence which Carl witnessed daily. Carl has attention-deficit and hyperactivity disorder (ADHD), but his doctors find it difficult to judge the correct levels of medication to enable him to negotiate successfully the school day. There are problems at school, and he has spent many hours in the school's 'time-out' facility, offering respite to his teachers and classmates. His mother and father are now separated, and Carl feels let down by his dad, who rarely agrees to see him and often cancels at the last moment. Carl feels rejected and takes this frustration to school. He is aware of his 'condition' and is willing to talk about it; indeed, he is keen to do so. The school is aware of his special needs and has made real efforts to take them into account. However, the situation is deteriorating, and some of his teachers feel he is 'getting away' with too much. They have questioned

▶

how much of his difficult behaviour is due to his ADHD, and therefore understandable, and how much is simply bad behaviour. This has introduced inconsistency into their approaches to him, and Carl is now confused and resentful of any intervention that is part of the school's behaviour code. Carl has been allocated a mentor, who meets with him regularly, and SMART targets for 'negotiated' behavioural improvement. To redress the school's apparently lenient approach to him, Carl has recently received a number of fixed-term exclusions so that he understands where the line is drawn. He has problems relating to other pupils and is consequently the subject of bullying, as other pupils react to his aggression and anger. They also resent the way teachers treat him differently and that he appears to be handled more sympathetically by his head of year.

Sunita

Sunita is a diminutive 11-year-old pupil who has struggled throughout Year 7. Her mother despairs over Sunita's refusal to go to school. Her attendance at junior school is just about satisfactory, although some concern had been expressed. Sunita's mother brings her to school, but the terrified child clings to the gate and cries. She begs her mother to take her home, promising to go to school 'tomorrow'. The learning mentor at the school has encouraged Sunita to enter the school on occasion, assuring her that she can spend the day alongside her, but the mentor knows this is not a long-term solution. When encouraged to go to lessons, albeit on a limited timetable, Sunita cries loudly, and her desperate appeals disturb others. When in school, she inevitably complains of stomach pains and headaches, and occasionally she has to be escorted to the toilet to be sick. The head of year is under pressure to improve Sunita's attendance, and the education social worker has been involved. Everything has been tried: encouragement and rewards, threats of court action, and the possibility of transfer to another school. Sunita has a very close relationship with her mother, and Sunita's crying has made it hard for her mother to maintain firm boundaries. At times, it is easier to allow Sunita to stay at home. Her mother is herself depressed and feels guilty about her role, as she had been hospitalised for a good part of Sunita's first few years of life. She remains intermittently unwell, and Sunita is worried that her mother will die as her aunt did.

Zoe

Zoe does not appear to be interested in school at all. Her Years 7 and 8 end-of-year reports showed an average student whose behaviour was within the normal range. Now, in Year 10, Zoe's coursework is non-existent. Constant phone calls home do not appear to make a difference. Her teachers are frustrated because they feel she is 'wasting her ability'. They are also concerned that her aggressive behaviour toward teachers and dinner supervisors is a bad example to others. Other students look up to Zoe and she occupies a position of power within her peer group. She has sometimes resorted to punishing those who challenge her superiority and status, by excluding them from the friendship group. Zoe spent just over a year on the child protection register when her 20-year-old brother interfered with her sister. While there was no suggestion that he had touched Zoe, social services established the risk. This affected the family in acute and profound ways. For Zoe, there were issues about her parents' failure to protect her sister and their defence of her brother, which hurt her deeply. The situation at home has reached crisis point and Zoe does not want to stay there. She habitually runs away. Zoe is self-harming and recently was hospitalised briefly after taking 10 paracetamol tablets in the playground, an event that caused great anxiety in the school. Periodically, Zoe goes a whole day without eating, causing her friends concern. Zoe is often in detention at school because of her 'attitude' and occasional rudeness. School uniform remains an issue, and the school is determined that she should dress the same as others. She has been excluded on three separate occasions for fighting and smoking. There is a suggestion, but no evidence, that she is smoking illegal substances.

Mohammed

Mohammed comes from what appears to be a very settled and caring home. He has two brothers who successfully attended his school without incident. Both gained good A levels, went to university and now have excellent jobs. Mohammed's parents show a great deal of interest in Mohammed, always attend parent consultation evenings, and comment in his 'school planner'. At school, Mohammed's behaviour is exemplary. He receives many 'credits' but rarely collects them. His attendance is faultless and he is often commended for the quality and accuracy of his uniform and preparedness for school, evidenced by his bulging pencil case. Mohammed is difficult to engage, although staff know he is highly articulate. He told his concerned form tutor that he has lots of friends, but he is rarely seen with them, preferring to sit alone in lessons and occupy the library at lunchtime. No one bullies him – he rarely attracts the attention of any adults or pupils in the school. He mostly goes unnoticed, although his teachers have high hopes that he will attain at least eight grade A–Cs. Mohammed is an asset to the school and his parents are proud of him and communicate their high expectations of him.

These four case studies represent the kinds of issues faced by schools every day. In all parts of the country, not just in the inner city, school staff grapple gallantly with young people whose behaviour is causing concern in various ways. To a large extent, the school's response is a behavioural one, because schools have traditionally operated in a behaviourist way, emphasising behavioural and cognitive approaches over models that place feelings at the fore. This may have a lot to do with the way we train teachers now, with less emphasis on philosophy and psychology, and more on practice and learning from experienced teachers in schools. We would do well to question the distinct lack of the 'pastoral' in the development of our teachers – a strange phenomenon when we consider the inherently human nature of teaching.

Reward and punishment, the bedrock of behavioural approaches, leads teachers sometimes to address a pupil's behaviour without really understanding the causes. The caring teacher who puts pressure on the underachieving pupil by establishing targets and offering rewards may, in fact, be adding to the stress and anxiety of that child. If we concern ourselves with the overt behaviour of young people, we end up punishing the sad pupil whose depression manifests itself as aggression. We may end up dealing with Carl in incoherent ways because we do not quite understand what is happening to him in the classroom and corridor, and fail to support him with the confusion, rejection or shame he may be feeling. We caringly put pressure on Sunita to get into school because we know 'what is best for her' without recognising the underlying causes of her fear, thereby exacerbating her anxiety all the more. We become frustrated and then angry with Zoe, whose behaviour challenges our own professional sense of worth. In doing so, we fail to support her through her understandable anger and her need to control her immediate environment and relationships. We focus on her violence without really understanding her pain and hurt. When she deliberately harms herself and threatens to take her life, she generates fear in the adults who care for her, and this leads to a belief that she 'needs help' of a kind that is beyond the resources of the school. The reality is that Zoe will indeed need additional support from other professionals, but she remains a student at the school until she is permanently excluded – the most likely outcome.

Mohammed represents the many students who may be experiencing a mental health difficulty but whose behaviour does not cause concern or, if it does, it remains a lower priority for an overstretched pastoral system. It would be difficult to guess what might be happening for Mohammed, but his withdrawn and isolated behaviour should be a concern for the vigilant teacher and the school that recognizes that early intervention prevents the development of more serious consequences in subsequent years.

Reflection box

- ◆ Thinking about the young people you currently work with, do you recognise any dimensions of the pupils described in these case studies?

- ◆ Looking beyond the behaviour, can you identify what might be happening for Carl, Sunita, Zoe and Mohammed?

- ◆ What might each young person be feeling?

- ◆ When reading the case studies, what were you feeling? Did you feel sympathetic to each pupil?

- ◆ Think about a time when you were at school and you felt confused, unhappy, anxious or even despairing. What did you need from your teachers and the adults with whom you came into contact?

Schools and mental health

Key points

Schools have an essential role to play in promoting young people's mental health, and teachers and other professionals working in schools are often in the front line. Schools should embrace these new responsibilities because attending to mental health and well-being will have a positive and profound effect on learning and pupil behaviour.

There is nothing new in the idea of being concerned about the mental health and emotional well-being of young people in schools. Teachers have always understood that young people bring a multiplicity of problems into the classroom, and that this affects their ability to engage with the curriculum in a purposeful way. The converse to this idea – that mental health difficulties act as a barrier to learning – is that mental health and well-being are a prerequisite for academic success. However, positive terms such as 'mental health' have not always been employed by school-based professionals, who traditionally have worked from a different frame of reference, using the currency of 'behaviour problem', 'disaffection' and 'dysfunctional'.

This is understandable: teachers and mental health professionals undergo completely different training and their role is differently defined. Katherine Weare (2003) has highlighted the differences between these two spheres of activity, seeing mental health professionals as being concerned with *individual troubled, troublesome and 'special needs' students*, while teachers have mostly been concerned with *developing a student's intellectual, logical, technical and sometimes creative powers, but rarely their emotional capacity*. She continues: *Those in education have tended to view what happens in the black box of 'mental health' as at best mysterious and medical, and at worst rather frightening and off-putting.*

Schools, of course, have a long history of trying to support teachers and help pupils in difficulty, and the roles of the educational psychologist, behaviour support teacher, social worker and, more recently, the learning mentor are testimony to these efforts.

There are those who argue strongly that it is the role of the school to educate. They insist that teachers and other school-based staff are not in the mental health business and that these concerns should be left to properly trained professionals with experience in the field. Schools, they assert, are there to teach our children and to facilitate learning. However, I believe it is important to see education as more than the passing on of knowledge and skills through a subject-based curriculum. In the push toward a greater emphasis on teaching and learning – however much that is to be applauded – it is important that we do not neglect what is at the core of education: a concern for a child's development in the widest sense.

This book celebrates a multiagency approach and collaboration between schools and mental health workers, but it also wishes to suggest that a concern for mental health and well-being is not incompatible with the traditional aims of the school, notably academic outcomes. Indeed, it is strongly argued here that any failure to address mental health issues in school will affect pupils' capacity to learn effectively. When young people feel supported, valued and secure, and have a sense of belonging, they learn better. When young people feel more robust and resilient, they are better prepared to cope with the problems they encounter. Put simply, happy pupils learn best. Also, where mental health difficulties are not addressed, there are consequences for young people and their families. The learning of other students, and sometimes the health and well-being of the child's teachers, can also be adversely affected.

The role of the school in exacerbating problems should not be overlooked. Students who persistently experience a lack of academic success due to an inappropriate curriculum are punished for their poor behaviour, which results from the unfortunate cocktail of emotional problems and school failure. The argument extends into a concern for the community in general, as young people with mental health problems are more likely to get into trouble with the police, cause difficulty in the neighbourhood and be users of mental health and social services in the future, with significant cost to all. The question, therefore, is not whether, but how schools should become more actively involved in mental health promotion and intervention.

The importance of the school in prevention of, and supporting pupils with, mental health problems was most recently brought to the fore with the publication of the guidelines, *Promoting Children's Mental Health Within Early Years and School Settings* (Department for Education and Skills (DfES), 2001). However, it appears that, for many schools, the school's influence was never substantial enough to effect change (Ofsted, 2005). Organisations such as the Mental Health Foundation, YoungMinds, the Samaritans, ChildLine, the British Association for Counselling and Psychotherapy (BACP) and other like-minded organisations have kept the cause alive.

This has not been easy, for despite a growing recognition of the importance of mental health and emotional well-being, secondary schools still appear, at the time of writing, to be preoccupied by fear of Ofsted inspections and the publication of formal academic outcomes such as GCSE results. These statistics bring teachers into competition with neighbouring schools and signal danger if a school appears to be failing, relatively, in these more measurable outcomes.

On a more optimistic note, the impact of *Every Child Matters* (DfES, 2004), and government legislation that places emotional health and safety as two of the five desired outcomes, could give impetus toward lasting awareness and change.

In her exploration of the *rift between the worlds of mental health and education*, Weare (2003) recognises that some the difficulties alluded to here may have to do with language. She writes: *In order for other professionals to feel more comfortable with what they often see as the frightening and rather medicalized world and terminology of 'mental health', there needs to be some mind-shifts about what mental health involves.*

She goes on to suggest that mental health has traditionally been used as a 'synonym for mental illness' and thus the preserve of mental health professionals. This may be referred to as the 'pathogenic' model. She also refers to the work of Antonovsky (1987), who advances a more positive concept, that is, a 'salutogenic' or wellness model that emphasises mental health promotion and emotional wellness. A whole-school approach that focuses on the creation of an emotionally healthy environment and a concern for the promotion of mental health is strongly advocated here and will be explored later in the book. However, such an approach may be insufficient alone. Whilst we recognise the importance of prevention, it is important also to recognise the high and increasing incidence of mental health difficulties among young people in our secondary schools. These are discussed below. What I am putting forward is a balanced approach, concerned with prevention but also showing a preparedness to support young people in difficulty, especially through early intervention.

Schools across the country are already doing a substantial amount of creative work with regard to mental health and well-being, although they probably will not refer to it as such. However, it may only be by recognising the nature and scale of the problem, and actually naming it, that we can move toward more coherent ways of working, both within schools and in genuine partnership with professionals drawn from other disciplines.

Reflection box

◆ At this stage in your reading, what mental health difficulties can you think of which might act as a barrier to learning?

◆ What words do you find yourself using for pupils who have difficulties in their home, school and personal lives?

◆ What do you think of when you read the words 'mental health'?

◆ What might be the consequences of not addressing mental health problems in young people – for the school, the home, the community?

◆ What does the word 'education' mean to you?

◆ What is your school already doing to promote mental health and support pupils with mental health difficulties? Make a list.

CHAPTER 2

Mental health and young people

Defining mental health

> This chapter discusses how:
>
> Mental health and mental illness are difficult to define accurately, but a school needs to be operating at a variety of levels if it is to prevent and respond to mental health problems.

The task of defining mental health and mental illness is a notoriously difficult one. The Mental Health Foundation, in *Bright Futures: Promoting Children and Young People's Mental Health* (1999), recorded:

> *If our views of children are ambiguous, our thinking on mental health is even more confused. The media feeds us images of 'the mentally ill' as unpredictable and dangerous maniacs who need to be locked up. At the same time Prozac, a drug intended to treat clinical depression, is deemed suitable by some as an aid to tackling the stresses of everyday life.* (p. 5)

Part of the problem lies in our historic use of the word 'mental', which has negative associations. Indeed, the word is used by both adults and children as a term of abuse. The link between the language of mental health and mental illness is explored later in this book when we look at the concept of 'stigma'.

Peter Wilson, former director of YoungMinds, addresses this problem, bringing a sense of clarity to the discussion. In his book, *Mental Health in your School: A Guide for Teachers and Others Working in Schools* (YoungMinds, 1996), he writes:

> *Mental health is often confused with mental illness, and as such quickly passed over to psychiatrists and other specialists to sort out. But in fact, mental health is simply what it says it is. It is about the health of the mind – that is, the way we feel, think, perceive and make sense of the world.* (p. 15)

Here, Peter Wilson is referring to mental health as a positive quality, reflecting a young person's capacity to live a full and rewarding life with confidence and sociability.

These sentiments echo the words of the World Health Organisation, which made an inspired early attempt to redefine mental health in positive terms way back in 1946. Health was described as *a complete state of physical, mental and social well-being, and not merely the absence of disease or infirmity.*

These ideas have been taken up by the Mental Health Foundation (1999), which sought to equate the definition of physical health as the absence of physical disease to the idea that mental health should be seen as more than *a narrow quasi-medical definition of the absence of diagnosable problems.* They emphasise the importance of mental health promotion for everyone. For a child, this means *being able to grow and develop emotionally, intellectually and spiritually in ways appropriate for that child's age* (p. 5).

A different perspective on our attempts to define mental health is to begin by identifying what actually constitutes mental health and emotional well-being. The DfES (2001) adopted the Mental Health Foundation's definition of children's mental health, which it had drawn from an NHS Health Advisory Service publication (1995), and saw the mentally healthy child as one who has the ability to:

- develop psychologically, emotionally, intellectually and spiritually

- initiate, develop and sustain mutually satisfying personal relationships

- use and enjoy solitude

- become aware of others and empathise with them

- play and learn

- develop a sense of right and wrong

- resolve (face) problems and setbacks and learn from them.

In the United States, the Surgeon General's *Report on Mental Health* (2000) defined mental health as *the successful performance of mental functioning resulting in productive activities, fulfilling relationships with other people and the ability to adapt to change and cope with diversity.*

Our list of mentally healthy characteristics is augmented by Helpguide, an organisation concerned with providing information on mental health (www.helpguide.org/mental_emotional_health.htm). The list includes:

- a sense of well-being and contentment

- a zest for living – the ability to enjoy life, laugh and have fun

- resilience – being able to deal with life's stresses and bounce back from adversity

- self-realisation – participating in life to the fullest extent possible, through meaningful activities and positive relationships

- flexibility – the ability to change, grow, and experience a range of feelings, as life's circumstances change

- a sense of balance in one's life – between solitude and sociability, work and play, sleep and wakefulness, and rest and exercise

- a sense of well-roundedness – with attention to mind, body and spirit

- creativity and intellectual development

- the ability to care for oneself and others

- self-confidence and self-esteem.

Some of the ideas may seem a little simplistic and too general to mean much, but I suspect that you may have already begun to consider them in relation to your own life and will begin to relate these characteristics to the young people you come into contact with in school. They are also useful indicators when we consider their opposites – an activity that may give us some insight into the meaning of mental health problems and mental illness.

A discussion as to the meaning of the words 'mental health problem' or 'mental illness' is equally important. A recent article in the *New York Times* (2005) by Benedict Carey explored the question as to where mental health ends and mental illness begins. He refers to two 'viscerally opposed camps'. These include doctors, who suggest a broad definition to include *mild conditions, which can make people miserable and often lead to more severe problems later*, and, on the opposing side, *experts who say that the current definitions should be tightened to ensure that limited resources go to those who need them the most and to preserve the profession's credibility.*

Case Study

Harvinder's behaviour is a cause for concern. His father was diagnosed with a severe mental illness three years ago and has been hospitalised on a number of occasions. The father does not live with Harvinder, his mother and his two brothers any more, although he still exerts a considerable influence over family affairs in a negative sense. His mother says that Harvinder is 'out of control' at home and has on occasion been violent toward her and his younger siblings. He has twice seriously damaged his home, and has ripped furniture and broken windows. At school, Harvinder is regularly removed from lessons for disruption but appears to show little remorse – even when his English teacher left the room in tears after one particular lesson. The school SENCO is at the point of beginning the statementing process but knows that this will take time. Harvinder is in Year 9, it is September, and his form tutor feels that he will not reach the end of the year.

In the preceding case study, does Harvinder have a mental health problem? Could he be suffering from a conduct disorder? Is he depressed and angry? Is he acting out his pain and confusion? Is this simply a classroom management issue? Should he be referred to an educational psychologist or CAMHS through his GP? Are there child protection issues? Schools around the country ask the same questions every day about young people in their care, and related discussions often have a feeling of helplessness and desperation about them.

Reference to the literature on 'abnormality' is often not helpful in attempting to define metal illness. Rosenhan and Seligman (1989) refer to elements of abnormality such as the 'violation of moral codes' and 'unconventionality', and they recognise that such definitions are social judgements. Similarly, Richard Gross and Rob McIlveen (1996) have concerns about such 'ideals', seeing them as 'value judgements' and 'bound by culture'.

Perhaps a more helpful concept is that of a continuum, with mental health at one end and severe mental illness at the other. Attempting to distinguish between what Katherine Weare refers to in her book *Promoting Mental, Emotional and Social Health: A Whole School Approach* (1999) as 'the well and the ill', we may feel more confident in understanding what might be found at these two extremes but less confident about what is in between. At one end might be normal anxiety, often regarded as necessary for everyday functioning, and at the other end, panic disorder that prevents patients from leaving their homes.

Harvinder's behaviour, which causes so much concern at home and school, is somewhere on that continuum. His anger and aggression are neither pathological nor seen as acceptable by the adults who come into contact with him. However, in many respects, his behaviour is understandable given his difficult circumstances.

In advocating the advancement of schools with a concern for the mental health of pupils and staff, the least desirable outcome is an organisation that is quick to label young people as having mental health problems – or one that is too quick to assume that behaviour is within the normal range for the period of adolescence, taking into account the additional stresses that young people experience from time to time.

It is important to see that we are all somewhere on that continuum, and there have been and will be points in our lives when we might require additional help. At one level, this might be provided by our close friends and family, but there may also be times when we ask for additional help from recognised professionals, such as a counsellor, psychiatric nurse or GP. If we apply this concept to our schools, the model fits well. It may be that Harvinder can be helped most effectively by the involvement of a caring teacher he has a relationship with and with whom he feels able to talk openly. There may be a mentor in school that he trusts. It may also be that a referral to social services will provide additional family support and perhaps offer further referral to a voluntary agency offering family work.

Harvinder's difficulty does represent a mental health issue, but it does not necessarily follow that he has a mental health problem or the beginning of a mental illness. Hasty referrals remove responsibility from individuals to professionals, and that is not always desirable.

A school that places mental health and well-being at the core of its aims can support Harvinder and his family at a variety of levels. It would provide the kind of healthy school environment where Harvinder feels safe and can thrive against adversity. It will be a school which recognises his difficulty and intervenes early, offering the kind of quality support which addresses some of his underlying issues whilst setting appropriate boundaries – so important when a young person's life appears to be spiralling out of control. However, this would also be a school that looks beyond his behaviour and recognises when outside help is necessary and understands what constitutes an 'intelligent' referral to other professionals, a matter which is addressed later in this book.

These ideas relate directly to the work of Tones (1981) as presented by Weare (1999), which offers a three-level model: the 'tertiary level', where a severe and recognisable mental illness has been diagnosed; the 'secondary level', which may be characterised by temporary mental illness or difficulty from which the person will probably recover; and the 'primary level', which may be seen as the wellness level.

Understanding that Harvinder's difficulties may be a mental health issue for the school and his family, affects our response to him. To focus on his behaviour alone is unhelpful.

Reflection box

♦ If Harvinder said he wanted to talk to you about home and school, what would you say?

♦ Can you add to the list of criteria that indicate that a person has good mental health?

♦ When you first read the criteria, did you find yourself reflecting on yourself or those close to you? What were you feeling?

♦ What do you consider to be 'abnormal' behaviour in a young person?

♦ Where are you on the mental health continuum? Has it been different at various times in the past?

How many young people in our schools suffer from a mental health problem?

Key points

There are a significant number of young people in the UK who are suffering from a mental health problem or illness. Most of these are also pupils in our schools.

In 1999, the Office for National Statistics estimated the population of the UK at just under 60 million. Children up to the end of Year 11 would represent over 20% of the population. The Mental Health Foundation (1999) suggests that at any particular time, up to 20% of children and adolescents may be experiencing psychological problems. Based on epidemiological studies of young people, the following figures are put forward as the possible incidence of mental health problems in young people:

■ 12% anxiety disorders

■ 10% disruptive disorders

■ 5% attention-deficit disorders

■ 6% specific developmental disorders, enuresis and substance abuse.

A lower figure, only 1%, is recorded for psychotic and pervasive developmental disorders such as autism.

Quoting the Office for National Statistics (2000), YoungMinds notes that over 10% of children and young people aged 5–15 years are affected by a significant mental health disorder. The figures for children of statutory secondary school age rise to 11.2%.

YoungMinds also records the following statistics drawn from a variety of sources:

■ Attempts at suicide are made by 2–4% of adolescents, of whom over 7.6 per 100,000 young people aged 15–19 years succeed.

■ Some 2–8% of adolescents experience significant depression.

■ Some 1.9% have obsessive-compulsive disorders.

■ Up to 2% have either anorexia nervosa or bulimia nervosa.

Similar figures are recorded by the organisation Mind (2001), which adds that self-harm affects 3% of adolescents and that the suicide rate in young men has risen significantly, by up to 75%, since 1982. YoungMinds argues that these distressing statistics may have risen to well over 100% in the last decade. It is also recognised that the incidence of conduct disorders is twice as common in boys as in girls, and for hyperkinetic disorders, such as attention-deficit and hyperactivity disorder (ADHD), the rate is even more significant, possibly up to four times as common.

Translating some of these figures into meaningful information for teachers and other professionals, YoungMinds calculates that in the average secondary school of 1000 pupils there are likely to be:

■ 50 pupils who are seriously depressed

■ 100 who are suffering significant distress

■ 10–20 pupils with obsessive-compulsive disorder

■ 5–10 girls with an eating disorder.

In addition, various other writers suggest that up to 100 young people in a similar school may be suffering from anxiety, while the figures for those abusing drugs or alcohol could be similarly large in inner-city areas.

Despite the legitimate concern that these figures may represent a medicalisation of behaviour problems and a tendency to label children in distress, they remain significant. My own experience suggests that in reality the figures could be higher, especially in relation to self-harm, eating distress, anxiety and depression.

This, then, is the task faced by schools. Wherever possible, we need to find ways to prevent these problems in young people from developing. We need to act early with our own school-based support systems and refer on to – and work directly with – mental health professionals where this is felt necessary and desirable.

Of course, any discussion of the incidence of mental health problems in young people belies the pain, suffering and despair that each brings to those young people and their parents or carers. We should also remember that it is not only diagnosable mental illness that invites us to be responsible about promoting mental health and emotional well-being in our schools; there are many young pupils experiencing a range of difficulties, often associated with the normal tasks of adolescence and growing up, that might also need our support. This is particularly so where normal development is potentially hindered or thrown off course by exceptional home circumstances.

Reflection box

◆ What were your thoughts as you read these statistics?

◆ Did any current or past pupils come to mind?

How do we know if a pupil has a mental health problem?

Key points

It is possible to identify a range of 'warning signs' that might help us to judge whether a young person has a mental health problem. These should be used with caution but nonetheless are indicators of concern.

For some, the period of adolescence represents the smooth transition from childhood to adulthood; for others, it is characterised by confusion, distress and conflict with friends and family. Those who parent, teach or come into contact with a teenager are often confronted by rebelliousness, irritability, moodiness and arguments. Sometimes adolescents can be aggressive and challenge authority. If we bear this in mind, it is not surprising that those who work with young people in schools sometimes find the job stressful: assembling up to 1500 adolescents in a single building in an attempt to teach and encourage them to learn can sometimes seem a bizarre idea.

Difficult behaviours are a 'normal' part of the process of growing up, becoming pubescent, seeking independence and reflecting on one's future. However, schools have a responsibility to support young people through this minefield as part of a wider commitment to the social education and emotional development of their pupils. In view of the kinds of statistics set out above, the reality is that some pupils in our schools may begin to develop mental health problems that, if left untreated, could develop into longer-lasting mental illnesses. The earlier a mental health problem is identified, the better the chance that the pupil can be supported and, if necessary, referred for treatment.

So how is it possible to distinguish between normal adolescence and the early stages of a mental health problem? The answer has something to do with how many warning signs are present, how persistent they are over a period of time, and the degree to which they are affecting the young person's individual and social functioning and the capacity to engage with learning.

Peter Wilson (YoungMinds, 1996) suggests that we ask ourselves the following questions when concerned about a pupil's emotional well-being:

- How extreme is the behaviour or attitude?

- How prolonged or persistent is it?

- Are there sudden changes in behaviour?

- How driven or out of control is the child?

- Is there a marked contrast in the way the child behaves at home and at school?

- How is the behaviour affecting other members of the school community?

It is important to remember that the presence of a variety of warning signs may not indicate a mental illness but may be a pointer to the need for additional support and intervention.

The comprehensive list of warning signs (see page 16) is included for your reference.

Photocopiable

Warning signs of mental health problems in young people at school

Feelings

- persistent sadness or depression
- pervasive feelings of hopelessness or despair
- often feeling anxious or afraid
- feelings of shame or guilt
- being irritable and angry for much of the time
- frightened that their mind is no longer under control
- marked frequent swings between negative and positive feelings
- significant mood swings that appear to be unrelated to events
- feeling bad about themselves or their appearance
- lacking in energy to do things and feeling tired much of the time
- feeling overwhelmed and troubled by their feelings.

Thoughts

- preoccupation with death and dying
- thoughts about suicide or hurting themselves
- overly rapid thoughts and ideas
- delusionary thoughts
- feeling of being another person
- paranoia — the belief that someone is watching them or seeking to harm them
- unexplained voices or hallucinations
- the belief that their lives are controlled by mystical or unreal beings or objects
- finding it difficult to make decisions
- limited understanding and difficulty with conceptual thinking
- thinking of themselves as bad or evil.

Behaviour

- being overly isolated or withdrawn
- avoiding social situations

© British Association for Counselling and Psychotherapy 2006 (BACP)

P *Mental Health in Schools* by Mark Prever (2006). Paul Chapman Publishing

- crying a lot, sometimes for no apparent reason

- having fears or phobias that affect ability to function normally

- showing loss of interest in leisure activities and inability to enjoy themselves

- experiencing sleep difficulties, including insomnia, sleeping too much and regular nightmares

- beginning to act in a sexually provocative manner

- drug use, alcohol abuse, crime or other undue risk taking

- speaking too quickly in a way that makes it difficult to understand them

- constantly dieting, missing meals and refusing to eat when others are around

- undergoing significant or rapid weight loss or gain

- making themselves sick or abusing laxatives

- playing with and/or starting fires

- communicating in ways that appear to be incomprehensible or not make sense

- lacking in energy, bored and lethargic

- often complaining of headaches, tummy aches or general illness

- attention seeking, hyperactive or restless

- behaving in a regressive way — starting to act in ways more common in younger children

- deliberate self-harming, including cutting, burning, hair pulling, head banging or biting nails until they bleed

- talking about suicide and periodically taking small quantities of pills, prescribed or otherwise

- being accident prone; often hurting themselves

- evidence of mutilating or hurting animals

- odd behaviours such as rocking or masturbating in public

- often starting fights with other pupils

- aggression toward adults and other pupils

- neglecting their appearance or personal hygiene

- adopting ritualistic, routine or repetitive behaviours that appear to be irrational

- regularly breaking the law with little regard for the feelings of others.

P *Mental Health in Schools* by Mark Prever (2006). Paul Chapman Publishing

Specifically in relation to school

- constantly worrying about academic pressure and school failure
- overly obsessive about their work
- having little motivation or sense of direction
- showing decline in school performance that fails to improve
- loss of interest in lessons or activities previously enjoyed
- becoming a workaholic
- avoiding making or maintaining friendships
- daydreaming and often off task
- difficulty concentrating; fidgeting and restless
- very low self-esteem and sense of personal worth; constant self-criticism, putting themselves down or making negative statements such as I'm thick; no one likes me; I'm stupid
- other teachers or pupils expressing concern about them
- significant decline in attendance
- refusing to go to school despite threats or encouragement
- appearing to be frightened of school
- often being the victim of bullying and appearing to place themselves at risk despite advice
- bullying others
- very demanding of teachers' time and attention.

© British Association for Counselling and Psychotherapy 2006 (BACP)

P *Mental Health in Schools* by Mark Prever (2006). Paul Chapman Publishing

CHAPTER 3

Risk and resilience

This chapter looks at:

Risk factors, those situations and events in a young person's life that increase their chances of developing a mental health problem. Resilience or protective factors are those that help a young person cope and survive in adversity.

As teachers and professionals working in schools, we sometimes find ourselves making comparisons among young people and their ability to cope with difficult situations in their lives. We may ask, how is it that two young people, both faced with similar problems in their lives, appear to cope so differently? One pupil seems to 'bounce back', whilst another seems to spiral into depression or anxiety, or appears out of control.

'Resilience' is an important consideration for those concerned with the mental health of young people in schools. Similarly, it is important for schools to be aware of those 'risk' factors that contribute to the likelihood of pupils developing a mental health problem or illness. The task of the school, therefore, is to find ways in which to minimise the negative effect of risk factors and build resilience in young people. The related concepts of risk and resiliency provide a fresh perspective on much of the work that good schools have been doing for many years. However, making these ideas explicit sets out a way of understanding our pupils and their difficulties with greater clarity and proposes an agenda for intervention with individuals.

The Mental Health Foundation (1999) suggests that a young person is more likely to cope with difficulty if there is a balance between risk and resilience. Where risk factors outweigh protective or resilience factors, a young person's life may become unmanageable. The Mental Health Foundation also attempts to explore the relationship between risk and protective factors, suggesting that it may be possible to:

- reduce the risk itself

- alter the exposure to the risk

- reduce the likelihood of a 'negative chain reaction' initiated by the risk factor

- promote self-esteem and self-efficacy in the young person

- create 'new and positive opportunities' and offer 'turning points' where a risk path may be 'rerouted'.

Risk factors

Risk factors will be considered in more detail in the next chapter, which sets out to explore the causes of mental health problems in young people. However, it is important to consider them here in relation to resilience, for, as the following pages will show, there is an obvious interplay and correlation between the two concepts. It has been suggested by the DfES (2001) that risk factors are 'cumulative'; that is, where there are more risks affecting a young person, there is a greater likelihood of difficulties developing. A similar negative indicator will, of course, be the 'severity' of the risk factor. Drawing upon the evidence submitted to the Mental Health Foundation Inquiry, *Bright Futures*, by Professor Peter Hill at the Hospital for Sick Children, Great Ormond Street, London, the final report offers the following broad statistics and informed calculations:

> *If a child has only one risk factor in their life, their probability of developing a mental health problem has been defined as being 1–2%. However, with three factors it is thought that the likelihood increases to 8%; and with four or more risk factors in their life the likelihood of the child developing a mental health problem is increased by 20%. We know, therefore, that the greater the number of risks, and the more severe the risks, the greater the likelihood of the child developing a mental health problem. (pp. 7–8)*

It would be useful here to consider risk factors under three headings, such as those identified by the Mental Health Foundation (1999). Inevitably, there will be overlaps.

Photocopiable

Risk factors

Factors within the child

- ■ genetic factors, although these alone are unlikely to cause mental health problems
- ■ sensory impairment
- ■ learning disabilities
- ■ communication and language difficulties
- ■ chronic illness
- ■ low self-esteem
- ■ religion, race and culture, including confusion as to personal identity
- ■ confusion over sexual identity
- ■ school failure
- ■ developmental delay that might include autism or Asperger's syndrome
- ■ early behaviour problems.

Factors within the family

- ■ parental mental illness, especially of an acute kind, such as schizophrenia, or of a chronic kind, as in a mother with long-term depression
- ■ family size; for example, having numerous siblings
- ■ family discord, conflict and disorganisation
- ■ family breakdown
- ■ violent or aggressive relationships where this leads to the child's experiencing fear or rejection
- ■ poor parenting resulting in inconsistent discipline, which might be considered as lacking in boundaries or being oppressive
- ■ abuse — where the young person has experienced physical, sexual, emotional abuse or neglect
- ■ parent criminality
- ■ parental drug misuse or alcoholism
- ■ bereavement and loss
- ■ parent education difficulties, such as school failure or learning difficulties

▶

P *Mental Health in Schools* by Mark Prever (2006). Paul Chapman Publishing

- lack of mutual attachment and nurturing during the early years
- low expectations leading to a lack of motivation and challenge
- too high expectations, leading to undue pressure and stress.

Community and environmental factors

- socio-economic disadvantage
- unemployment affecting family income and parental emotional well-being
- housing problems, including overcrowding or homelessness
- poor neighbourhood, including living in an environment of decay or inner-city decline
- racism and discrimination
- peer factors, including negative peer influences associated with crime, anti-social behaviour or drug misuse, or social isolation as a result of peer rejection
- membership of an at-risk group, as in looked-after children, young carers and refugees
- bullying resulting in fear, isolation and possibly self-hatred
- experiencing a traumatic event, perhaps being involved in war, an accident or terrorism, or being the victim of a crime or violence.

P *Mental Health in Schools* by Mark Prever (2006). Paul Chapman Publishing

Resilience

For some time, researchers have been interested in learning about resilience, believing that if we can understand more about such protective factors, we might be able more effectively to prevent mental health problems developing in young people – or at least reduce their impact.

An understanding of resilience and protective factors is important because it suggests ways in which interventions can be made by the school and other professionals to increase pupils' ability to cope with change and survive adversity. The key task for schools is to find ways to translate these concepts and ideas into practical action and intervention.

An excellent representation of the nature of the concept of resilience is provided by Julia Vellacott (2005), a psychotherapist working in London:

> *Resilience is not a matter of absolute strength. Like a tree that bends in the wind but does not break, resilience involves the ability to return to shape; to suffer but not to shatter, not to become so stuck in a defensive position where there is an impoverishment of personality. Indeed, the struggle involved in hardship may lead to growth created out of that hardship.* (p. 18)

As adults, we often value life experience in another person, and it is sometimes argued that it is a necessary part of growth and development. In some way, life experience contributes to the growth of maturity and better prepares us for life's challenges. It is important to note, however, that in some cases where a child has experienced significant trauma – as in the case of chronic abuse – 'resilience' alone may not be sufficient, and additional care may be needed as part of the recovery process. In a similar way, it should be understood that resilience does not 'inoculate' a young person from the effects of severe trauma, and in many situations there may be deep and long-lasting scars, sometimes continuing into adulthood.

Photocopiable

Resilience factors

Factors within the child

- being a girl
- having a good vocabulary and use of language
- having normal cognitive development
- emotional literacy
- being a 'good' baby
- ability to maintain attention and concentrate
- secure early attachments
- being attractive to others by appearance, temperament or personality
- high self-esteem and sense of worth
- a sense of humour
- empathy
- developed problem-solving skills including the ability to think clearly, make plans and ask for help when necessary
- an internal locus of control and a belief in one's own ability and self-efficacy
- positivity in the face of adversity
- ability to establish and maintain friendships
- a sense of meaning in life, including goals and direction
- self-awareness and a positive sense of self
- developed social skills and competency
- a sense of autonomy and the desire and ability to carry through tasks alone
- flexibility and the ability to adapt
- ability to cope with change
- ability to move successfully between different cultures
- good resistance skills, where the young person develops the ability to resist peer pressure and risk-taking behaviour
- a sense of sexual identity
- awareness of the needs of others.

P *Mental Health in Schools* by Mark Prever (2006). Paul Chapman Publishing

Factors within the family

- a strong relationship with at least one competent, loving and caring parent
- parents who have sought pre- and postnatal care
- regular family income and employment
- continuity of parenting, where there has been no long separation from a parent
- a family where anger, conflict and stress is managed well
- child receiving quality time from parents and other family members, as in working and playing together
- not having to compete with more than four siblings
- having older siblings whom they can turn to
- clear boundaries set and expectations about behaviour expressed clearly
- avoidance of personal criticism; discipline focusing on the behaviour rather than the young person
- an extended family including grandparents, uncles and cousins
- a family where love, compassion and affection are demonstrated
- positive and mature family communication
- education valued and supported
- child involved in family decision making
- reading at home encouraged
- safe and healthy home environment
- having access to a positive familial role model
- the young person's skills, assets and qualities noticed and explicitly valued with encouragement to build on these
- strong family faith, religion or belief system.

Factors within the community and environment

- good housing
- a good neighbourhood where the young person is not overexposed to drug misuse or violence
- positive peer influences, especially those that reject anti-social behaviour

© British Association for Counselling and Psychotherapy 2006 (BACP)

P *Mental Health in Schools* by Mark Prever (2006). Paul Chapman Publishing

■ the community provision of opportunities for good health and social care, employment, recreation and childcare

■ community recognition the achievement of young people locally and nationally.

School protective factors

■ at least one significant and caring relationship with an adult in school

■ high expectations of academic success

■ high behavioural expectations and firm and clear boundaries

■ positive school climate and high morale among staff and pupils

■ extensive extra-curricular programme including sports

■ opportunity for active participation in the life of the school

■ curriculum that is structured, thematic and experiential

■ curriculum that recognises that children learn in different ways

■ concern for promoting the self-esteem, independence and self-efficacy of pupils

■ teachers offering time and space to listen

■ school providing welfare, mentoring and counselling as part of the formal pastoral system

■ teachers and other adults in school model caring relationships and communication

■ school encouraging young people to have a sense of connectedness and belonging

■ pupils valued equally regardless of difference

■ school demonstrating commitment to physical and emotional health, and healthy lifestyles and sexual attitudes encouraged

■ conflict managed well

■ pupils' achievements valued and celebrated

■ clear policies on anti-bullying and drug misuse

■ well-established programmes in personal and social education and citizenship

■ active sex education policy and programme for personal relationships and sex education

■ caring, empathic teachers and support staff

■ teachers showing genuine interest in and concern for pupils' learning and well-being

P *Mental Health in Schools* by Mark Prever (2006). Paul Chapman Publishing

■ school providing professional development opportunities for staff

■ teacher encouragement of the development of pro-social behaviour

■ school encouraging parental involvement

■ school making opposition to injustice and discrimination explicitly clear.

P *Mental Health in Schools* by Mark Prever (2006). Paul Chapman Publishing

Simply 'being a girl' may seem an odd factor in measuring resilience. Generally, girls may be stronger emotionally, and this may result from the fact that girls share their feelings with family and friends, more readily than boys. There may even be inherited or genetic differences between boys and girls.

The list, of course, is endless and highlights all those ideas and practices that constitute a caring and effective school. However, the list also highlights opportunities for action with regard to mental health promotion. These will be discussed more fully in a later chapter. It should be noted that the potential for school intervention is not confined to this final (school) section. Teachers and other school-based professionals are in a position to encourage, develop and support many other protective factors within the child, family or school. We are not in a position to change a child's gender, effect change with regard to inadequate early attachments, change the early nurturing experience, find jobs for unemployed adults in the family or even encourage parents to have fewer children! We can, however, build self-esteem, and help pupils develop friendship skills, develop a sense of autonomy and learn to resist negative peer pressure. In the context of family and community, we can support families in distress, advise on behaviour management, encourage parents to recognise their child's achievements where these are hidden, and generally encourage a good working relationship with the school. With regard to the community we can counterbalance negative peer influence and either directly, or in association with other statutory and voluntary agencies, support families facing practical problems in relation to housing or health problems within the neighbourhood. Of course, this is nothing new; schools have been supporting and encouraging parents and pupils for many years. However, understanding these actions in the context of mental health promotion and intervention points the way to a more coherent and comprehensive whole-school approach.

Reflection box

- ◆ Can you identify from your experience a pupil who appears to thrive against all adversity?

- ◆ Consider a number of risk factors mentioned in this chapter. How might the risk be reduced? Can we affect exposure to that risk or prevent a 'negative chain reaction'?

- ◆ In what ways is your school already working to increase resiliency in its pupils?

- ◆ Think of a pupil you know. How might the school increase or improve his or her protective resilience?

- ◆ Reflect upon those protective factors which may have contributed to your own resilience.

CHAPTER 4

What are the causes of mental illness in young people?

This chapter looks at:

The causes of mental illness in young people. The causes are complex and often the result of a number of interrelated factors. Some of these are of direct interest to schools, struggling to understand and work with the young people in their care. Some groups of young people are particularly at risk due to specific circumstances.

There is, of course, no simple answer to this question. It is likely that a mental illness in a young person is caused by a complex interplay of biological, psychological and environmental factors. Mental illness rarely has one cause; it is more likely to be multifactorial. What is clear is that mental illness should not be seen simply as a weakness of character or the result of poor nurturing. Similarly, recovery from a mental illness cannot be viewed as a matter of being strong willed or of young people 'pulling themselves together'.

Biological factors

Here, mental illness is seen as a sign of a physical or organic disorder. Biological abnormality can arise in a variety of ways. Observation and studies of some mental illnesses suggest that mental health problems appear to have a genetic origin and run in families. In this sense, mental illness is seen as a matter of inheritance, whereby some DNA material containing our genetic code is passed on from generation to generation. Whilst it is unlikely that ideas and images are inherited, it is believed that parents' genes contain 'instructions' to future generations, determining not only looks and a tendency toward physical illness but also the way we think and feel. Genes alone rarely cause mental illness; more likely, genetic factors are triggered by trauma or environmental factors. In other words, it does not necessarily follow that, simply because there is mental illness in the parent, the child will inevitably inherit that problem; it just makes it statistically more likely.

Some mental illness can be attributed to chemical imbalances. Neurotransmitters are the body's chemical messengers that convey information from neuron to neuron and facilitate communication in the brain. Where these chemicals are out of balance, we may see signs of mental illness. It is well known that deficiencies in serotonin can affect moods, precipitate anxiety and alter sleep patterns.

Other biological causes include infection of the nervous system, damage to the brain as a result of drugs or alcohol, and pollutants such as lead and other toxic chemicals. The brain can also be affected by severe physical trauma such as head injury, metabolic disorders affecting chemical balance, endocrine and hormonal problems, dietary deficiencies and the ill effects of medication.

Psychological factors

Psychological factors include those concerned with personality and temperament. These may predispose a young person to a mental health problem. For example, a child with an anxious disposition may be more likely to develop an anxiety disorder, be a school refuser or suffer from depression. Some mental illness is associated with early attachment problems. Mental illness may also be triggered by acute or chronic trauma, such as physical, emotional or sexual abuse or neglect, domestic violence and bullying. Inevitably, the loss of a parent, family member or close friend can have a profound effect on a young person's mental health and well-being. Other psychological factors include those associated with self-image, ideal self, actual self and subsequently self-esteem.

Environmental factors

These might include:

- living in poverty
- divorce or separation of parents
- school-related factors such as academic pressure or exam stress
- sexual or racial harassment
- dysfunctional families
- transitions and life changes such as moving schools
- drug and alcohol misuse.

In fact, many of the risk factors discussed in the previous chapter are, by definition; contributory factors in mental illness.

Space does not permit me to explore all the factors that might affect a pupil's mental health, but below I wish to look in a little more detail at those which may be of direct concern to schools in particular. These include:

- child abuse
- domestic violence

- divorce and separation

- bullying

- academic and exam stress.

Also, there are a number of pupils who may belong to 'vulnerable' groups whose circumstances may be contributory to or exacerbating factors in the mental health of young people. These include pupils from black and other ethnic minority groups, refugees and asylum seekers, pupils with learning difficulties, young people who have experienced chronic childhood illness, and children with alcoholic or drug-dependent parents. By way of example, I consider below the following groups of pupils who may face additional and complicated risk:

- children whose parent suffers from a mental illness

- looked-after children

- bereaved children

- gifted and talented pupils

- gay and lesbian pupils.

Child abuse and mental health

Child abuse, whether sexual, physical or emotional, is a major mental health issue. My own experience of working with young adults who were abused as children has shown that the effects can be debilitating, pervasive and long-lasting – a view that is supported by many studies.

It is not unusual for schools to make periodic referrals to social services where there is evidence of physical abuse. Physically abused pupils are more likely to become anxious, as they live in fear of a recurrence of the violence. Such anxiety may result in stress, often leading to depression. Physically abused children may become overly aggressive toward adults in the school, and their peers. This may eventually lead to more serious emotional and behavioural problems and school failure.

Emotional abuse includes adult behaviours such as rejecting, isolating, insulting, humiliating, constantly criticising, threatening and belittling. It may also involve the lack of, or withdrawal of, love and affection and the necessary conditions for normal social and emotional development.

Emotional abuse serves to devalue children's self-esteem, inducing feelings of inferiority and poor self-worth that leave children with a negative outlook on life. They may come to view themselves as useless and blameworthy. Emotionally abused pupils may also display signs of overt or passive aggression or may become shy, withdrawn or overly compliant. They may become highly dependent on or demanding of adult attention, with significant consequences for relationships at school. The pupil who is abused emotionally may develop compulsions, obsessions and irrational fears, and may show cruelty to others. It could be argued that the cumulative effect of long-lasting and persistent emotional abuse upon a child can be more dangerous to that child's mental health than periodic physical abuse or even sexual assault.

Many people have written about the effects on young people who have been sexually abused, including Draucker (1992) and Sanderson (1995). Some of the effects may be immediate, whilst there may also be a legacy later in life, particularly if there has been absence of quality support.

A young person who has been sexually abused may experience a deep sense of shame. Shame is a powerful emotion that can have a deeply corrosive effect in the long term. The pupil may experience a number of powerful feelings such as guilt, confusion, denial, grief and anger. Other effects of sexual abuse might include the onset of depression and anxiety, as young victims struggle to make sense of their shattered world.

Young people who have been sexually abused are more likely to engage in deliberate self-harm and attempt suicide, whilst the development of eating disorders and drug abuse is also common in abused children. One of the most significant and alarming effects of abuse is that the young person may suffer from post-traumatic stress disorder, characterised by flashbacks, nightmares and compulsive thoughts, which may last for years if left untreated.

Sexual abuse will often have a profound effect on the pupil's interpersonal relationships, which may become disturbed and dysfunctional. Relationships with close family members and friends become strained, especially if the abuse occurred within the family itself. In the long term, abuse may interfere with the pupil's ability to form warm and trusting relationships with a partner and there may be a fear of intimacy. It is a recognised phenomenon that there is an increased likelihood of the young person forming similarly abusive relationships into adulthood. Needless to say, there may be subsequent problems with engaging in sexual activity with a partner and there are links with promiscuity, prostitution and other forms of sexual exploitation. The abuse may have a distorting effect should the victims of abuse later become parents themselves, and for many young people there remains the fear that they might repeat the behaviour of those that have abused them.

Finally, there may be associated cognitive effects on the young person. In school, they may begin to fall behind with their work, lose motivation and behave more erratically, either withdrawing into isolation or acting out in a confrontational or aggressive way.

How domestic violence affects the mental health of a young person

Domestic violence occurs where physical, sexual or emotional abuse is inflicted on a partner. In most cases, this is the woman, although there is increasing evidence that men may also be victims of domestic violence. It would be incorrect to assume that all domestic violence involves actual physical assault. Often it begins with more subtle forms of emotional violence and neglect, including threats, put-downs, and comments and actions designed to embarrass, demean or humiliate. There may be a variety of forms of verbal aggression and attempts to control the victim's environment and relationships, before gaining momentum toward violence against property and subsequently against the person, in the form of pushing, shoving, slapping, punching, biting and kicking. In some cases, weapons may be used. Domestic violence may also be associated with sexual violence where one of the adults is coerced, pressured or forced into sexual activity with the other partner. Domestic violence often leads to serious injury and sometimes death. The Royal College of Psychiatrists (1999) notes that as many as one in four women are abused by their partner. They also suggest that violence is more likely where there are children in the family, and often begins during pregnancy and after the birth of the child.

Children and adolescents in our schools who witness domestic violence can be deeply affected by their exposure, and the effects may continue into adulthood, compromising future mental health and well-being. Clearly, the effects of the violence will depend upon a number of factors, such as the nature and severity of the violence, how long the young person has been exposed to it, and the child's age and degree of resilience. There may be additional complicating factors if the children have been victims of abuse themselves by the same adult, or if they have been involved directly in the abuse of the same parent. There may be secondary consequences of the abuse, including the diminished ability of the abused parent to offer the child support and the use of alcohol or drugs as coping mechanisms.

Pupils who have been exposed to domestic violence are sometimes in a constant state of anxiety, fear or even terror. They may experience continuous psychological pain, feeling sadness and a profound sense of the loss of the family and relationships they feel they should have. They may begin to feel helpless and without a sense of hope or purpose. They may fear their own mortality or become concerned for the life of the abused parent. There may be contrasting emotions of guilt – expressing a sense of responsibility for the violence and anger – and fury at one or both of the parents involved. There may be some ambivalence about relationships, and the pupils may feel 'in the middle' – torn both ways and unsure about where loyalties lie. They may begin to hold contrasting feelings simultaneously, such as dependency and need at the same time as fury and rage.

Sleep may be affected as the young person is woken by the violence or by nightmares. Such pupils begin to view the world as unsafe, and they find it hard to trust, having been let down by the adults in their lives. Their world now becomes threatening, all-consuming, hostile and unpredictable. Nothing seems the same any more; their world is turned upside down.

Boys often cope more aggressively, acting out their pain and confusion. Girls may also be aggressive, and their behaviour may become a cause for concern, but they are equally likely to internalise the problem, becoming more depressed and anxious. Both boys and girls may develop difficulties in resolving disputes with siblings and friends – conflict being the inevitable result.

The pupils may exhibit regressive behaviours, retreating into the ways of a younger child. Conversely, they may take on an adult, caring role, seeing themselves as the protector of the abused or violated parent and responsible for the safety of younger siblings.

The Royal College of Psychiatrists (1999) also refers to complications in later life, including the idea that the children may become abusers or victims themselves. They argue that children learn from the example set by their parents; boys may learn to be violent to women, and girls may come to see that *violence is inevitable and something you just have to put up with*.

The emotional impact of divorce and separation on young people

The Royal College of Psychiatrists (1999) estimates that up to 50% of all children in the UK will see their parents divorce or separate. This means 150,000 children of school age will be separated from one parent. When these figures are translated to the school setting, the implications are significant.

Pupils whose parents divorce or separate are more likely to experience difficulties at school. Behaviour is affected, with the pupil possibly becoming more aggressive; work suffers; and there may be changes in attendance patterns, through an increase in either condoned absence or truancy. The school's disciplinary machinery comes into play, as it struggles to manage the young person's behaviour that threatens to spiral out of control.

There are very practical consequences of a marriage break-up, including financial constraint as parents sometimes have to cope with reduced income. There may be house moves involved and a general lowering in the standard of living of the remaining family. Families might be torn apart and siblings split between former partners. There are also, statistically, likely to be issues typical of reconstituted families, as parents find new partners and a former parent may be replaced by a step-parent in law or simply by way of cohabitation. All of these significant life changes can happen within a short period of time, leaving the pupil disoriented, confused and insecure.

The *Times Educational Supplement* (2003) explored the impact of 'parents at war' in their series 'The Issue'. They noted how pupils may be affected prior to, during and after the split, leaving some young people with emotional and behavioural problems. They also alerted us to the potential difficulties when the split is not managed in an amicable way with both parents keeping an eye on the emotional needs of the children affected:

> *And if the separation is adversarial, the effect can be even more devastating and long term. Children can get caught in the middle, often used by one parent to get at the other … . When it is adversarial, the child may be drawn into the conflict, forced to hear endless criticism and hostility from each parent about the other or be asked to take sides or find fault.*

It follows that the mental health of a young person can be affected by parents becoming consumed by the split themselves and consequently being less emotionally available to the children involved. At school, a pupil may become more dependent, attention seeking or needy. It may well be that the child who experiences divorce experiences the same range of emotions as a child who has lost a parent through death.

Children of separating parents will experience a wide range of emotions. These include denial, as the children shut down their feelings in an attempt to avoid the acute feelings of grief and loss. This may lead to silence in the child that can be mistaken by parents and schools as acceptance, resulting in children being denied the kind of emotional support they need. Feelings 'bottled-up' are more likely to show themselves in other ways, as through angry outbursts and the bullying of other pupils.

Family break-up often results in feelings of shame and guilt. The pupil may feel different from and inferior to other young people where the family remains intact. Guilt comes on account of the mistaken belief that they have caused the split-up. There may well be anger too, directed at the parent whom they feel is responsible, or both. There may be emotional confusion as the young person faces decisions around loyalty and betrayal, leaving the young person torn apart.

Children may have feelings of deep insecurity as they enter a period of rapid change, as relationships and routines become disturbed and no longer predictable. Children may also fear abandonment, believing that having lost one parent, they may lose the other. However, linked to this may be feelings of rejection, one parent appearing to walk away from them. This may raise questions of self-worth and value, with inevitable consequences for the child in school, as confidence is lost and alternative ways of feeling good are sought. This may take the form of looking out for other pupils whose behaviour suggests that they, too, might be in pain – making the young person feel less judged and more accepted.

Pupils may lose a sense of direction and become disaffected from school. They may become isolated and the victims of bullying themselves. They may worry about the future and what might happen to them, or become consumed by beliefs that their warring parents will be reconciled and reunite, returning to the status quo. The pupil may also develop signs of anxiety, and younger children may start to become ill, complaining of stomach-aches and headaches and generally feeling unwell. Some young people may experience panic and be physically sick, with many trips to see the school nurse.

As with any discussion about the mental health consequences of life events, the reality is often complex and affected by other risk and resiliency factors, and some children appear to cope better than others. It should also be noted that separation or divorce may be preferable to unhappy parents living together 'for the sake of the children' or because economic factors prohibit living apart. Swan-Jackson (1997) notes how, for some of the young people in our schools, divorce or separation may be a relief, especially where continuous conflict or domestic violence may be involved.

Bullying and mental health

Bullying remains a persistent and high-profile concern of most schools. It may be seen as:

- hurtful behaviour where harm is intended

- occurring over a period of time, possibly of a repetitive or serial nature

- involving an imbalance of power where victims are often unable to defend themselves.

Bullying takes a variety of forms. It can be physical, involving hitting, punching, tripping up, pushing, hair pulling, kicking, spitting or throwing objects at another person. The physical element may be indirect, taking the form of inducing other, more confident and powerful pupils to assault the victim. Bullying may be verbal and include insults, name calling, spreading false and malicious rumours, and talking about family members in rude or offensive ways. Verbal bullying may also take the form of malicious phone calls and attempts to extort money or possessions. Bullying can of course be non-verbal, such as excluding people from the group, or taking their belongings and hiding them. Non-verbal bullying also takes the form of 'dirty looks', or implying physical threat by gesture. It may include racial or sexual harassment. More recently, cyberbullying has involved the use of computers and mobile phones. Unfortunately, there are almost unlimited ways in which young persons may use their powers and relationships to bully others.

For most young people in our schools, bullying is a transient experience. In terms of mental health consequences, these are more likely to be significant if the bullying is severe and persistent over a long period of time.

Most profoundly, bullying is an attack upon a pupil's self-esteem. This may have been a significant factor in why the young person was initially targeted for victimisation by potential bullies, and now is compounded by the negative attention. Pupils who are bullied may begin to feel worthless and ashamed, seeing themselves as a failure, inferior to others and valueless. They may begin to feel incompetent and unattractive or even ugly, questioning their looks and acceptability to others.

Pupils may begin to feel anxious or panicky; they may start refusing to go to school. They begin to live in fear of the bullying and hide themselves away. This constant emotional strain may cause physical symptoms, and health may suffer as a consequence. Sleep patterns may become disrupted, and the pupil may begin to experience bad dreams or nightmares.

Bullying often has severe repercussions for social relationships; victims of bullying report feeling excluded and isolated. This affects their ability to form trusting friendships with other pupils. At school, victims may find it hard to concentrate and they may become moody or irritable. Sometimes, displaced anger is directed toward other 'less powerful' pupils or adults in the school. Constant anxiety, low self-esteem and social isolation sometimes lead to depression in young people. They may come to question their reason for living, contemplate their own death and develop suicidal ideas. They may begin to harm themselves. The media often report the ultimate effect on the mental health of a victim of bullying, when victims attempt to take their own life or succeed in doing so – possibly the most devastating tragedy for both schools and parents.

Academic pressure and exam stress

It is a discomforting thought that schools, as well as doing their best to support pupils' emotional development and well-being, may in fact be a contributing factor to the mental ill health of the young people in their care. A key area where schools could usefully examine their own curriculum, policies and procedures is that of academic outcomes, particularly formal attainment, as measured by exam success. As government piles the pressure on schools, these targets and expectations are transmitted to our pupils via teachers who themselves feel the pressure to achieve the targets set by school leadership teams – who perhaps feel the pressure themselves most acutely.

There is growing concern about the effects of academic and exam pressure on our young. The National Institute for Clinical Excellence has ranked exam pressure alongside other problems, such as bullying, bereavement and abuse, as a cause of mental health problems in young people. This itself has been triggered by concern about the increasing prescription of antidepressants for young people. Such a concern is reiterated by Smith in her article 'Britain: Teenagers Driven to Depression and Suicide by Exam Pressures' (2004), which refers to evidence that appears to link exam stress with the use of psychiatric drugs and teenage suicide. She also records how the children's charity ChildLine has reported significant increases in the number of young people using its website or calling to complain of exam pressure. In an article in the *Guardian* (13 September 2004), Madeleine Bunting, also asks us to consider the idea that *we're raising kids to pass exams, but not face the world*, adding that they are now paying for their lack of emotional resilience.

Many studies about stress argue that *a little stress is a good thing*, serving to motivate our young and helping them to concentrate their energies on academic goals. But, clearly, too much stress can have negative effects on a pupil's emotional well-being. Continuous assessment has been recognised as taking the pressure off final exams, but it places new stresses on our pupils, particularly on those who are conscientious and who are taking the full range of examination subjects at GCSE level or above.

Young people may not consciously recognise stress in themselves, and they may show the pressure in other ways. They may become irritable and experience eating distress or sleep disturbance. They may become obsessional about routines and develop a concern for perfectionism. They may begin to overwork, lose a sense of life balance and become emotionally exhausted. Pupils under pressure may not know how to ask for help or even recognise the pressure they are under. They may become nervous and agitated, and develop many of the physiological symptoms of stress, including ulcers, digestion problems and increased heart rates. The young person's mind may begin to race, and memory may become impaired. They may find decision making harder, as their concentration is affected. They become moody and on edge much of the time.

At the heart of the pupil's anxiety is the fear of failure. They are concerned about letting other people down, particularly parents, but they also fear the humiliation they feel would come with not achieving their goals. Stress and anxiety, unceasing over long periods of time, is linked directly with depression and, as we have seen above, with suicide.

Exam pressure itself may not be the only cause of mental ill health in pupils in our schools. Competition, pupils not being able to achieve academically, banding, setting, streaming, workload and homework may all be areas a school needs to consider in any discussion of creating a mentally healthy school environment.

Examples of young people at additional risk

Children who have a parent suffering from a mental illness

Growing up in a family can be difficult at the best of times, but it is particularly challenging for those pupils in our schools who have a parent at home suffering from a mental illness. Of course, mental health issues are not new to most families, and many young people experience times when one or both parents may be depressed, anxious or more stressed than usual. In most situations, these phases are short-lived, and with the help of the GP or a specialist, difficulties can be overcome and more normal functioning resumed. However, some young people have a parent whose illness extends over a long period of time and is severe and debilitating. The problems may be most complicated when a parent is suffering from a diagnosed psychotic illness, such as schizophrenia, with long periods of separation due to the hospitalisation of the parent. In these circumstances, children in the family face additional risk.

Of course, in some cases, the risk may already be present in a biological sense, with some mental illness – or inclinations to it – already proven to be carried on from one generation to another via genes. There is a greater likelihood that a young person will suffer from ADHD, depression, schizophrenia, and bipolar and other personality disorders when these have been diagnosed in a parent.

A young person whose parent has a mental illness may face a number of additional practical problems that need to be negotiated, each with an emotional consequence. Additional responsibilities beyond those that might be expected of an adolescent may emerge, including caring for the parent who is unwell or the partner. Younger brothers and sisters may have to be protected and cared for to compensate for the under-functioning parent. Children themselves may be neglected or even physically abused. This is most likely where drugs and alcohol present mental health issues in themselves, or where they are associated factors. Indeed, parental mental health remains a significant factor in the number and type of referrals made to social services under child protection guidelines. In the most extreme circumstances, young people have been seriously injured by a mentally ill parent; in rare cases, they have died from the violence inflicted upon them.

Returning to the idea of neglect, it follows that parents who are clinically depressed or have an obsessive-compulsive disorder or a more serious personality disorder are unlikely to be able to support a child's own emotional development. Parents consumed by their own mental health issues may be less available for their own growing child and less able to support them psychologically and practically. The parent may display unpredictable or disconcerting behaviours, leaving the child frightened and confused. Young persons who see their parents hearing voices, experiencing an episode of paranoia, or saying things that appear to be incomprehensible and without logic or reason, may become terrified at what they cannot make sense of. If a young person witnesses a parent's suicide attempt at first hand, the sense of terror and insecurity could be all-consuming.

Fortunately, the chances of a child dying at the hands of a mentally ill parent remain small, but more significant is the potential long-term damage to a child's psychological health and emotional well-being. Pupils in school whose parents are suffering from a mental illness may find it particularly difficult to seek help, as they may be infused with a sense of responsibility or guilt. They probably will feel a sense of shame; in particular, young persons may be ashamed of their parents' behaviour, perhaps when they visit their school or when friends call. Parents' behaviour may cause embarrassment if it takes the form of bizarre and unpredictable actions. Pupils may also be concerned about their own mental health, fearing that they may end up with the same difficulties. This can take the form of anxiety or more acute panic attacks that may serve to confirm to the young person their belief that they are losing control of their mind. The perceived instability of the parent may also cause pupils to reflect upon themselves, and they may face confusion and an identity crisis of their own. They also become more vulnerable to any minor crisis or life difficulty, the children's reduced resources rendering them impotent and unable to make decisions.

Pupils may develop a range of relationship difficulties, often ending up withdrawn or separated from others in the school and outside. They may find it difficult to establish and maintain lasting friendships, hindered by suspicion, lack of trust and low self-worth.

At school, pupils may become absorbed by their work in an attempt to divert feelings from the reality they face each day. They may become aggressive as they unsuccessfully deal with their anger. If the pupils are unable to understand the nature and extent of the parent's illness, they may be less than sympathetic, and overt or repressed anger may be the expression of fear and resentment.

Looked-after children

The term 'looked-after children' specifically refers to those young people who are 'accommodated' by the local authority and therefore under its 'protection'. Sometimes this is with the consent of parents or carers. Some children may be subject to care orders and placed in residential accommodation. Young people may be placed in foster care, and in some cases be subject to a care order but still spend significant time at home. According to the *Times Educational Supplement*, on 31 March 2003, just under 70,000 young people were being looked after by local authorities – which represents around 0.5% of young people up to 18 years of age. There are normally more boys than girls who are 'looked after'. The numbers are rising particularly in the under-10s.

Almost by definition, young people who find themselves in care will already have experienced a wide range of difficulties, including the loss of a parent or abuse of some kind, and many will come from dysfunctional homes. In addition, it is clear that the emotional effects of moving from home into one or more new environments and having to establish relationships with unknown adults is quite substantial. The Mental Health Foundation (2002a) tells us that looked-after children are far more likely to develop mental health problems than those young people living in 'settled' homes. They also suggest that these problems often go unnoticed and help is not given. They refer to the 'traumatic upheaval' of being moved from their own homes, under whatever circumstances. They also mention that some young people fail to settle in their new environment and may experience mixed feelings about what has brought them to this point:

> *Some young people, especially if they have been moved from their own home, may find it hard to settle and may feel torn or even guilty at being removed from their family, however abusive or neglectful (although some may feel a sense of relief because of their changed circumstances).* (p. 2)

The link between being looked after and the incidence of mental health problems is made clear by the Office for National Statistics (2003). In a survey report, they suggest that among young people aged 5–17 years who are in local authority care, up to 45% may be suffering from a mental health disorder. The report found that among young people aged 11–15 years, the prevalence of mental disorders for children looked after by local authorities, compared with children from the private household survey, were as follows:

- emotional disorders: 21% compared with 6%

- conduct disorders: 40% compared with 6%

- hyperkinetic disorders: 7% compared with 1%

- any childhood mental disorder: 49% compared with 11%.

According to the *Times Educational Supplement* (18 June 2004a), more than one in four children in residential care for a year or more have a Statement of Special Educational Needs; this compares with 3% nationally. They also added that such children are up to 10 times more likely to be excluded from school than their peers.

Children in the care of their local authority are more likely to have health-related problems and are more likely to smoke, drink alcohol and abuse drugs, and be the perpetrator or the victim of bullying at school. They often experience difficulties with the curriculum at school and generally do less well in their GCSEs, and many will leave school with almost no formal qualifications.

The feelings of a young person in local authority care will be confused and complex. Often they will experience a cocktail of rejection, insecurity, anger, shame and loss. These and other emotions can contribute to depression and aggression. They may also feel the stigma of no longer living at home. This may lead to a sense of embarrassment and low self-esteem.

My own experience of working with looked-after young people is that their feelings sometimes appear to get out of control, and peers become especially important, as if they offer some kind of attachment to others. These pupils can be overwhelmed by feelings that remain raw and current. The pupil sometimes begins to truant from school and engage in risky behaviours. School becomes less important except for the social contact it provides. In some cases, schools fail to recognise the tension and upheaval in the young person's life and 'will' them to find routine and security in school. The young person's perspective may be different, and, rather than developing a sense of belonging, the pupil becomes alienated and disaffected.

Bereaved children

In my work in schools, I am often surprised and saddened at the number of young people who have lost a parent through death. Sometimes we tend to see death as occurring in older age and forget that parents in their 30s and 40s may lose their life through illness, accident or suicide.

Bereavement is a normal part of life; all of us will experience the grief associated with the death of a loved one at some point in our lives. By the time pupils get to secondary school, they may already have had such an experience, most probably through the death of a grandparent but sometimes a parent or sibling. Sometimes friends die prematurely and the tragedy is felt by pupils who knew the young person and by the whole school community.

Attempts have been made to make sense of the bereavement process and identify the 'stages' of grief. The loss of a loved one is normally described by words such as shock, denial, anger, guilt and sadness. Eventually, we expect a young person to move through a number of stages toward 'acceptance' and a return to normal life.

When adults experience the death of a loved one, it is believed that they will already have experienced the feelings associated with loss and may be better able to cope with the bereavement. For a young person losing a parent, this may be their first taste of the many emotions associated with grief, and they may well be unprepared.

Of course, everybody will react differently to a death and, as the Royal College of Psychiatrists (2002b) notes, children often react differently from adults. They also cite a range of other factors that might affect a young person's response to the loss of a significant person in their lives. These include the child's age and level of understanding and the particular circumstances of the death. They suggest that a traumatic or sudden death may be harder for a young person to cope with than a death that brought relief from prolonged suffering. They also imply that there may be other family factors such as the impact of the death on other family members, and how this might impair the quality of support offered to the child. In some families, the death may not be discussed and children may therefore be unable to express their feelings. They may even attempt to protect the feelings of remaining family members by remaining silent. Such deep, unresolved emotion may begin to manifest itself in unexpected ways, and these behaviours may not be linked by the school to the original loss.

Loss of this kind can never be explained in simple, theoretical terms. In my experience, the death cannot be considered in isolation from the child's relationships, past, present and future. For example, a young person in conflict with a parent who dies may be filled with a deep sense of guilt, with matters unresolved and little prospect of these being worked through to a point of resolution or reconciliation. Adolescence is a difficult time for many young people, and the loss of a parent at the time of seeking independence can appear to derail normal change and growth.

Most of the young people in our schools, with appropriate care and unhurried support, will negotiate the mourning process successfully, reaching a point where they have 'come to terms' with their loss. Whilst feelings may persist into adulthood, they begin to fade and become proportionate and probably end up as a sense of 'missing out' on the relationship that would have been. They may also have treasured memories of the lost loved one and always have a repository of sadness deep within them that emerges when another person experiences bereavement or when they read a book or watch a film.

However, unresolved or complicated grief can cause mental health problems in young people that can persist into adulthood, with serious consequences for future relationships and social functioning.

Some young people are not able to grieve, or start but do not carry on, and feelings of denial and disbelief can continue for long periods of time. Depression is a direct consequence of mourning that did not begin or was cut short. Chronic depression may begin to pervade all aspects of the young person's life during the daytime at school, at evenings and weekends at home, and at night in the form of disturbed sleep patterns. Eating routines may be affected, and eating disorders may be triggered as the young person seeks to regain control of a life that has lost its shape and focus. Depression may be evidenced by the physical appearance of sadness in the young person, apathy and unwillingness to engage with life and others. Appearance may suffer, too, with little concern for what others think about them. Pupils may become overly concerned about their own mortality or fear for the lives of other loved ones. In this way, the young person enters a destructive period of consuming anxiety – and physical symptoms such as feeling sick, or having a headache or stomach-ache may soon follow.

The pupil's behaviour may take a downward turn, and school performance may slip below the norm expected for that young person. Encouragement, reward, sympathy and coercion may serve only to heighten some of the feelings already being experienced. Some behaviours may appear to be regressive and child-like. Prolonged sadness may take the form of withdrawal from the social world, and children may appear 'stuck', possibly still believing that their loved one will return at some time in the future; that they have not really died. Long-term depression may become debilitating and hard to recover from without professional help. Sometimes children's grief may become distorted, and they become incapacitated by acute anger, self-blame or guilt – emotions that will affect current and future relationships and the young person's sense of self. Young persons may also consider taking their own life in a vain attempt to be with the lost person again.

The mental health of gifted and talented pupils

Pupils in schools who have been identified as having additional gifts and talents are, of course, ordinary young people, and their developmental needs are the same as those of other children.

It also follows that gifted and talented young people are equally susceptible to the risk factors discussed in an earlier chapter. The gifted and talented pupil may have an alcoholic parent, suffer abuse or have parents who divorce or separate.

There is some discussion of whether gifted and talented pupils are more likely to demonstrate greater resilience because they share some of the skills and qualities associated with resilient people, such as the ability to solve problems. High intelligence is also seen as a protective factor. However, much of the literature relating to gifted and talented children highlights the particular social and emotional needs of these young people, and the potential for mental health difficulties if their needs are not addressed. Some of these are discussed below.

Gifted and talented pupils are often perfectionists and have a strong ideal self that they strive incessantly to become. They can be overly self-critical if they do not meet the standards they have set for themselves. Paradoxically, their abilities become less of a cause for self-congratulation and more often the beginnings of low self-esteem and self-criticism. Academically, such pupils may be plagued by a fear of failure, a fear made real by the impossible goals set by the young persons.

Gifted and talented pupils live and work under the constant pressure to be extraordinary. This may cause stress and anxiety as they experience the need to demonstrate how able they are. They may also be under pressure real or imagined, from parents and family, but equally stressful. This sometimes results in these young persons dominating classroom activity and sometimes even putting other children down by their display of brilliance, or, more directly, in the form of derogatory comments. Within friendship groups, they may attempt to take control and organise others. Such behaviours will generate resentment among peers and friends.

The pupil may also be seen as a loner by others, because work, study and the development of given talents removes them from the peer group and leaves less time for social interaction and behaviours normally associated with adolescence.

An inappropriate and undemanding curriculum can lead to boredom in school and behaviour problems, and underachievement may be the consequence. These pupils may develop special learning needs, as when cognitive ability outstrips their ability to communicate their thoughts and ideas in writing. Such advanced thinking, hindered by a lack of motor skills, may lead to a degree of frustration and irritability. Matters may be further complicated if the pupil is at different stages of development, not only intellectually, but also physically and emotionally.

The young persons may also fail to find like-minded friends and may become isolated. They may begin to experience the tension between being comfortable with their identity and their desire to fit in and conform. The school may begin to identify 'problems' in non-conformist behaviours that represent the pupil's need to feel distinct and different. There is evidence also that in order to 'fit in' and avoid isolation or bullying, gifted and talented pupils may deliberately fail to achieve in an attempt to keep their qualities hidden and therefore make themselves more palatable to their peers.

Most gifted and talented young people are well adjusted and go on to thrive socially and academically, but some do not, and begin to present with emotional problems such as depression and anxiety, leaving parents and the school confused, disappointed and helpless.

Gay and lesbian pupils

As most of us are aware, the task of growing up in the modern world is filled with difficulty, and the period of adolescence is a particularly difficult time for many young people as they strive toward adulthood. During this time, teenagers begin to develop a sense of their sexual selves, and for many this can be a difficult process. For gay and lesbian pupils in schools, this can be a very stressful journey. Many gay and lesbian young people are fortunate to have the support of family and friends and perhaps a sympathetic adult in school, and they may also have developed an inner resilience that will sustain them through this difficult time. For others, this may not be the case, and the school years can have a profound and devastating effect on their mental health and well-being. It is likely that lesbian and gay young people are statistically more likely to experience depression and anxiety and are overrepresented in groups that self-harm or attempt suicide. These mental health problems are to do not with sexual identity but with the reactions of other and wider societal attitudes. Homophobia can lead to the hurtful use of language and sometimes even threats or actual violence. It remains difficult for these pupils to express openly their sexual feelings without fear of ridicule or, worse still, actual bullying. The result is that, in schools today, gay and lesbian young people often feel isolated and fearful, and often carry a deep sense of guilt or shame. Often schools make the assumption of heterosexuality, and many aspects of the curriculum, including, of course sex education, serve to heighten feelings of not belonging, or rejection.

Reflection box

◆ Consider other 'vulnerable' groups such as black and ethnic minority pupils, and refugees and asylum seekers. What additional factors may contribute to mental health problems in these young people?

◆ Take one of the vulnerable groups discussed in this chapter, namely, children with a mentally ill parent, looked-after children, the bereaved child, and gifted and talented pupils. How can your school reduce risk and build resilience in these young people?

◆ Apart from academic pressure and exam stress, how else might a school contribute to mental health problems in young people?

◆ Mental health problems may develop as a result of the complex interplay between biological, psychological and environmental factors. Do you see mental health problems in young people as the result of nature or nurture?

CHAPTER 5

Specific mental health problems and young people: how schools can help

This chapter looks at how the:

Many myths and inaccuracies about mental illness affect our behaviour toward young people. These need to be challenged. Young people are affected by the full range of mental health problems, many of which require specialist professional intervention. However, these young people most often attend our schools each day, and there are a variety of ways in which we can support them.

Misconceptions about mental health are widespread and are found even among professionals working with young people in schools and related settings. It is important to be aware of the facts and to separate these from the fiction in order to end discrimination and treat young people with the respect and dignity they deserve. Sound information also helps teachers and other school professionals to avoid the consequences of mental health problems going unrecognised. It also avoids the kind of misunderstandings that result in poor decision making about the correct course of action to take.

This chapter serves as an introduction to the many kinds of mental health problems encountered in schools. Some are rare. The average member of staff is unlikely to come into contact many times with a young person suffering from, for example, psychotic illness. Others are more common and strike fear into pastoral staff, who feel deskilled and out of their depth – and equally frustrated by what they perceive to be too few routes for referral and access to professional advice.

What follows is a brief look at some of the mental health problems affecting young people. Clearly, each can be touched on only in summary form, and the reader may wish to refer to specialist books for more information. However, I have given more weighting to the following mental health problems, believing them to be among the most common in secondary schools and to cause most concern to teaching and pastoral staff:

- Asperger's syndrome

- attention-deficit and hyperactivity disorder (ADHD)

- conduct disorder

- depression

- eating disorders

- school refusal

- self-harm

- suicide and attempted suicide.

For each of these mental health problems, I provide a brief description, some of the ways in which it can be recognised and how it is usually treated. This section also includes ways in which the school can manage the young person's problems more effectively and offer help and support. The problems are addressed alphabetically. Certain identified pages may be photocopied for training and information purposes.

Asperger's syndrome
What is it?

Asperger's syndrome is a neurobiological developmental disorder sharing some of the same characteristics as autism. It is more common than autism, but remains relatively rare. The symptoms are less severe than those of autism and appear to affect boys more than girls. Children with classic autism are likely to be educated in special schools or units, whereas those with Asperger's syndrome are often successfully taught in mainstream schools. However, educating a pupil with this disorder in secondary school presents significant difficulties. (See photocopiable pages 46–7)

Attachment disorder

It is often stated that the first few years of a child's life are the most critical in terms of social and emotional development. These are the bonding years when young children form an emotional attachment to their primary caregiver. It follows that the quality of parenting at this time in the child's life will determine future development. During these years, the child has needs and the parent's or carer's ability to recognise and meet these needs is very important.

Sometimes things go wrong. If a child's bonding with a significant adult is interrupted or absent, attachment disorders may develop. Abuse or neglect, extended separation due to hospitalisation, post-natal depression and major changes in family life, as well as the caregiver's own unmet attachment needs in childhood, may disrupt this process of bonding and lead to problems later in the child's life.

Photocopiable

How do you know if a pupil has Asperger's syndrome?

Pupils with Asperger's syndrome will have particular difficulties with social interaction and communication. They may:

- be viewed as eccentric by their peers

- say things which appear to be inappropriate

- take comments literally, leading to misunderstandings and arguments

- have difficulty with language, as with the social context of speech and in the style of delivery

- have difficulty understanding the 'rules' of conversation and interrupt or end conversations inappropriately

- make comments which are deemed too personal or offensive

- be reluctant to accept change

- exhibit rigidity of thought and obsessional behaviour, often carrying out ritualistic actions

- have a preoccupation with a particular interest or topic that appears abnormal

- find it difficult to work collaboratively with others

- have problems with imaginative play

- not understand social 'rules' or 'cues', sometimes misinterpreting situations and causing offence

- have difficulty reading emotions in others and display little empathy

- have difficulty interpreting non-verbal behaviours, including the facial expression and body language necessary for good social interaction

- be above average in intelligence and hold a great deal of knowledge about a subject but may have difficulties with concepts, ideas and comprehension

- have difficulty concentrating on some tasks and be easily distracted

- have difficulty with transferable skills.

What can the school do to help?

Here are some ways in which a school can manage and support a pupil with Asperger's syndrome:

- Keep the classroom a consistent and predictable learning environment.

© **British Association for Counselling and Psychotherapy 2006 (BACP)**

P *Mental Health in Schools* by Mark Prever (2006). Paul Chapman Publishing

■ Have clearly established classroom routines.

■ Connect with the pupil's area of interest and try to relate this to the curriculum.

■ Make use of visual materials which aid the pupil's understanding.

■ Keep the classroom an orderly place with clearly established rules and expectations of appropriate and inappropriate behaviour.

■ Apply consequences consistently.

■ Express rules in positive terms.

■ Offer a place of 'safety' at break and lunchtimes as these can cause anxiety.

■ Be aware of the possibility of bullying.

■ Avoid the stress induced by change by preparing the pupil.

■ Involve the young person's peers so that they have a better understanding of the condition.

■ Teach social skills to the pupil.

■ Keep spoken language simple, concrete, precise, clear and literal, avoiding double meanings, sarcasm and too much use of metaphor.

■ Encourage and reward each attempt to communicate effectively.

■ Recognise that homework is a problem and offer in-school support.

■ Avoid demonstration of anger and authority, which can lead to stubbornness and conflict.

P *Mental Health in Schools* **by Mark Prever (2006). Paul Chapman Publishing**

The attachment-disordered pupils may find it hard to form loving intimate relationships. They may become mistrustful of other people and learn to manipulate relationships by acting in a charming but superficial way. The young person may become indiscriminately familiar with strangers and clingy. Other features of the disorder include lying, despite ample evidence of the truth; being destructive to self and property; and sometimes cruelty to other children and animals. The pupil may be controlling, hypervigilant, attention seeking, lacking in affection or empathy, and blaming of others, and have difficulty with authority. Such pupils may believe that they are unworthy of love and affection and have low self-esteem. They may be less able to cope with stress and frustration and act in defiant or aggressive ways toward adults and peers. They are more likely to engage in anti-social activity, risky behaviours and addictions.

Attention-deficit and hyperactivity disorder (ADHD)

ADHD is characterised by persistent difficulties in paying attention and impulse control, and hyperactivity. Affecting 3–5% of the school population, it is one of the most common of the childhood behaviour disorders. ADHD is a chronic disorder that begins in infancy and persists into adulthood. It can have a profound effect on the child's family, the school and the wider society. It is linked to school failure, exclusion and poor vocational outlook. ADHD remains controversial: some question whether it can be effectively diagnosed or treated, and claim there is little evidence of neurological differences. (See photocopiable pages 49–50)

Bipolar disorder

Known more commonly as manic-depressive illness, bipolar disorder is a serious mental health problem characterised by abnormal shifts in mood. In contrast with everyday changes in emotion, the young person suffering from bipolar disorder experiences larger mood swings, and euphoric feelings are disproportionate and appear to be unrelated to events in that young person's life. Bipolar disorder is one of the few mental health problems which can be harder to treat in children and adolescents than it is in adults. The illness can sometimes be difficult to detect, bearing in mind the topsy-turvy world of adolescence and the range of emotions experienced at this time. However, bipolar disorder can have devastating effects on children's lives at home, school and with their peers.

Manic symptoms include inflated self-esteem, elated moods, excessive energy and grandiosity, decreased need for sleep (patients often go for days with little or no sleep), talking incessantly and loudly with frequent changes in topic and theme, inattention, hyperactivity, distraction, uncontrolled thoughts and ideas, engaging in risky behaviours likely to cause physical harm, and over-attention to sexual matters by way of thoughts, feelings and behaviour.

Depressive episodes may include periods of deep sadness and irritability. Other symptoms associated with such depression include loss of interest in activities once enjoyed, disturbed sleep patterns, low self-esteem and feelings of worthlessness, over- or undereating and thoughts about suicide.

All this represents serious implications for schools, who will obviously find it hard to manage mood swings and teach a pupil who is extremely high or low at any given time.

Photocopiable

How do I know if a pupil has ADHD?

The following are some of the main characteristics of ADHD. Pupils may:

- become bored after a few minutes

- be easily distracted

- become restless, fidget and have difficulty sitting for long periods of time

- be selective about what they concentrate on, often giving most attention to activities they enjoy

- have difficulty with taking turns and may dominate some activities, such as the use of a computer or games

- have difficulty with giving close attention to detail

- have difficulty following verbal instructions

- have difficulty listening when spoken to

- be distracted by normal stimuli

- be forgetful and disorganised

- leave tasks incomplete

- talk incessantly, sometimes mistiming interruptions

- like to climb and run about inappropriately, sometimes engaging in risky behaviours

- act without considering consequences

- blurt out answers before the question is completed

- display tantrums, including slamming doors and throwing furniture.

How is ADHD treated?

ADHD is normally treated by drugs known as stimulants, including methylphenidate (also known as Ritalin), dextroamphetamin (Dexedrine or Dextrosat) and pemoline (Cylert). It may appear strange that drugs designed to stimulate brain activity should be administered to a young person when more calming drugs would seem to be needed. This is because these drugs are designed to affect those parts of the brain that control behaviour and regulate activity. Parents I have worked with report significant improvements in behaviour, but the drugs are not a cure. Concern has been expressed that these and other related drugs have been used with children displaying general behaviour problems not necessarily associated with ADHD. Drugs are often used alongside behavioural and more holistic therapies.

P *Mental Health in Schools* by Mark Prever (2006). Paul Chapman Publishing

ADHD: What can the school do to help?

- Seat pupils at the front of the room with their back to the rest of the class, but do not exclude them from their peers.

- Arrange for medication to be taken safely and regularly in school but avoid drawing attention to this.

- Encourage self-monitoring of behaviour.

- Be patient and avoid being overly critical.

- Offer regular praise and encouragement, recognising success and achievement.

- Make work interesting, new and highly motivating to increase attention.

- Establish clear rules and consequences that are frequently reinforced verbally and visually.

- Minimise unnecessary distractions and be aware of sounds in the room which might affect the pupil.

- Include variety in the lesson, especially incorporating more kinaesthetic-style lessons.

- Give calm, specific and clear instructions, maintaining eye contact.

- Check for understanding.

- Establish routines and keep changes and alterations to a minimum.

- Negotiate clear achievable targets for work and behaviour and celebrate success at whatever level.

- Use teacher attention as a reward for positive behaviour.

- Move around the classroom and be clearly visible to the pupil.

- Make sure all resources and equipment are readily available to the pupil.

- Be warm and empathic, and attempt to look beyond the behaviour to connect with children trying desperately to control their behaviour, win approval and find success.

P *Mental Health in Schools* by Mark Prever (2006). Paul Chapman Publishing

Conduct disorder

Conduct disorder is a complex group of behavioural and emotional problems found in children and adolescents. Pupils with these disorders may have difficulty following rules and behaving in the socially acceptable ways normally expected of their peer group. Often, their problems are perceived by parents, schools and peers as wilfully bad or delinquent behaviour and treated as such. Negative reactions from adults to the young person's behaviour fuel the difficulties. The causes of conduct disorder appear to relate to susceptibility to genetic factors and a range of genetic influences such as inconsistent behavioural expectations at home. These might include overzealous discipline, abusive relationships between parents, loss or grief, physical or emotional abuse, criminal behaviour of parents or siblings, and the negative influence of the peer group. It is often associated with oppositional defiant disorder, which is seen as the precursor to later and more difficult conduct disorders in adolescence. (See photocopiable pages 52–3)

Depression

Most of us would like to think of childhood as being a carefree time. However, the truth is often very different. At one time, we thought that depression largely affected only adults and that 'feeling down' or 'sad' was an inevitable part of the growing-up process. There is now a huge literature contradicting this view, and it is generally accepted that young people do suffer from depression, a potentially serious mental health problem that affects how young persons think, feel and behave. Depression is more than just 'the blues' and, left untreated, can lead to school failure, alcohol or substance abuse, and even suicide. The Royal College of Psychiatrists (2002d) estimates that depression affects two to three of every 100 teenagers. My own experience of working with young people in a variety of settings suggests that the figures may now be even higher. (See photocopiable pages 54–5)

Photocopiable

What are the signs and symptoms of conduct disorder?

- bullying, threatening and intimidating behaviour
- fighting, sometimes using weapons (bricks, bottles, sticks) without regard to the danger of causing injury
- rude and unacceptable language
- cruelty to helpless animals and pets
- vandalising property
- forcing someone into unwanted sexual activity, including sexual assault and rape
- setting fires for excitement and with the intention of destroying property
- theft, including shoplifting; theft possibly involving face-to-face contact with the victim but also burglary or breaking into cars
- uncooperativeness and disregard of rules set by parents and the school
- mistrust and fear of adults
- truanting from school
- running away from home for prolonged periods
- lying as a natural reaction to criticism, to avoid blame or to manipulate and influence friends, family and the school.

How is it treated?

In some cases, conduct disorder may coexist with other childhood mental health problems such as ADHD and depression, and these may need to be addressed simultaneously, perhaps with the use of medication. Sometimes the child is offered anger management and other cognitive-behavioural therapies designed to improve communication, problem-solving skills and impulse control. Where there are associated learning difficulties, special needs input may be appropriate. Where resources exist, family therapy or parenting education may be offered to help with management of the young person within the home.

What can schools do to help?

- Understand this condition and focus on the child, not the challenging behaviour.
- Avoid power struggles; remain calm and avoid becoming overly angry with the pupil.
- Focus on the pupil's good behaviours, not the negative ones.

© British Association for Counselling and Psychotherapy 2006 (BACP)

P *Mental Health in Schools* by Mark Prever (2006). Paul Chapman Publishing

■ Offer choice.

■ Offer constructive feedback about behaviour within the context of an established relationship.

■ Use classroom approaches which focus on activity.

■ Model effective communication and conflict-resolution skills.

■ Set clear expectations for behaviour and make consequences fair, proportional and consistent.

■ In the classroom, set clear and achievable goals and reward any movement along the continuum.

■ Use behaviour-modification schemes designed to motivate, such as 'token economies' and reward-linked behavioural contracts.

■ Build trust, show interest and listen.

■ Build self-esteem.

P *Mental Health in Schools* by Mark Prever (2006). Paul Chapman Publishing

Photocopiable

What are the signs and symptoms of depression in young people?

- persistent sadness that will not go away
- feeling irritable, worthless, guilty, hopeless and empty
- under- or overeating
- irregular sleep patterns and frequent tiredness
- difficulties with concentration
- recurrent thoughts of death or committing suicide
- boredom
- wanting to be alone much of the time
- friendship difficulties
- extreme sensitivity to criticism, failure or rejection
- inability to find interest in activities previously enjoyed
- using alcohol or drugs to control moods
- lack of energy; fatigue
- regular complaints of symptoms such as headache, backache and stomach-ache that have no physical cause
- low self-esteem
- falling off in school performance
- poor school attendance
- volatility, aggression, tantrums, anger and rage
- talking about and actually running away from home
- crying a lot.

How is it treated?

The good news is that depression is, more often than not, treatable, especially where there is early diagnosis, treatment and support. Sometimes doctors prescribe medications such as antidepressants. Their use remains controversial, but it often appears to relieve symptoms by affecting brain chemistry. Young people may also be offered counselling or psychotherapy in order to provide a safe place to talk about underlying issues. Cognitive-behavioural therapy may also be arranged, offering the young person the chance to challenge some of the negative, self-deprecating and erroneous thoughts that may be at the root of their sadness.

P *Mental Health in Schools* by Mark Prever (2006). Paul Chapman Publishing

How can schools help?

- Develop a warm, caring and supportive school environment.

- Recognise that depression can be very real — not a sign of weakness but a potentially serious mental health problem.

- Ensure that symptoms of depression are not mistaken for laziness or poor behaviour. This emphasises the importance of effective listening and attempts to understand the pupil in context.

- Be a good listener, making time and space to talk with young persons and encouraging them to express their feelings.

- Be non-judgemental, warm and empathic.

- Encourage the reluctant pupil to seek help.

- Introduce programmes into the curriculum designed to encourage pupils to learn about and express their emotions more effectively.

- Monitor pupils closely.

- Deal with bullying swiftly and effectively.

- Ensure that every pupil in the school has at least one adult who knows them well.

- Observe pupils closely and be alert to signs of depression, especially changes in mood and behaviour.

- Encourage and facilitate friendships in pupils who appear isolated.

- Encourage participation.

- Be alert to any talk of suicide; take these comments seriously. This means contacting parents and the pupil's GP.

- Know your limitations and those of the school and refer on, as appropriate, to mental health professionals.

P *Mental Health in Schools* by Mark Prever (2006). Paul Chapman Publishing

Eating disorders

Eating disorders are associated with eating problems and an overwhelming obsession with weight. These emotional disorders take a variety of forms, but the most common are those concerned with anorexia nervosa, which involves depriving oneself of food in order to become or remain thin. It often involves a degree of distortion about body image. Not eating may also be associated with the abuse of laxatives and a tendency to over-exercising. Bulimia nervosa involves binge eating and a loss of control followed by feelings of guilt and the need to purge the body of food consumed. This may involve laxatives or, more commonly, induced vomiting or the abuse of diuretics. Compulsive or binge eating is similar to bulimia, but the young person becomes overweight, not attempting to avoid excess calories. As many as 10% of school-aged girls (the figure is lower for boys) may experience eating distress, and some of these may go on to develop a full-blown eating disorder. Eating disorders can have serious medical consequences, but they are seen as the physical expression of emotional distress and turmoil. In some ways, they may be seen as a means of coping with distressing or unacceptable feelings that threaten loss of control. (See photocopiable pages 57–8)

Generalised anxiety disorder (GAD) and other anxiety disorders

GAD is a mental health problem affecting many young people and adults. A degree of anxiety or worry is normal and helps us plan our lives and avoid doing things that might harm us. However, GAD is excessive, exaggerated and unrealistic anxiety that is more persistent than ordinary worry. Young people with GAD worry about everything and anticipate disaster. It leaves them feeling out of control. GAD is 'general' in the sense that it does not focus on one particular aspect of the young person's life but is all encompassing and pervasive. Its many physical symptoms include insomnia, gastrointestinal problems, headaches and high blood pressure. It can have profound effects on the sufferer's personal and social life, sometimes becoming so disabling and debilitating that the young person ceases to function effectively, and relationships and schooling begin to break down.

GAD is one of a number of anxiety disorders, including *social phobia*, which denotes anxiety about social situations that appear to the sufferer to increase the risk of embarrassment or humiliation, especially where they might find themselves the centre of attention; *panic disorder*, which involves a loss of control and disturbing physical symptoms triggered by conscious or unconscious thoughts that imply a threat to health and security; and *separation anxiety*, which may be normal in infants and toddlers but is likely to be developmentally inappropriate in adolescents and young adults. *Somatoform* disorders, such as *hypochondriasis*, involve fear of having a serious or fatal disease, despite evidence to the contrary. It may be seen in the many, often younger, pupils who present in school with physical symptoms, such as stomach-ache, headache or nausea, for which no medical cause can be found. Young people are also prone to develop the full range of *phobias* that represent a powerful but irrational fear of an object, living thing or situation. These can sometimes be so debilitating that they interfere with the young person's capacity to lead a normal life. *Obsessive compulsive disorder* (OCD) and *school phobia* are discussed on page 59.

Photocopiable

What are the signs and symptoms of eating disorders?

- continual refusal to eat or maintain normal body weight
- noticeable weight loss
- wanting to be left alone
- preferring to eat alone or in secret
- hiding food
- excessive or unnecessary exercising, often bound by rigid and ritualistic regimes
- irregular menstrual periods
- obsession with parts of the body such as the size of buttocks, waist or stomach
- expressed fear of gaining weight or becoming fat
- excessive dieting
- fussiness about food
- dehydrated or poor skin condition
- lack of interest in food
- regular sore throats, mouth infections or swollen glands
- overeating
- sleep problems
- the need for perfection
- frequent denial of being hungry
- dishonesty and lying, especially about food
- becoming manipulative
- often going to the toilet during and after meals
- tooth decay, sore mouth and gums
- overinterest in food, cooking and calorific values
- dizziness
- problems with concentration
- need to feel 'in control'
- skipping lunch at school and missing meals at home
- abdominal pains or constipation

© British Association for Counselling and Psychotherapy 2006 (BACP)

P *Mental Health in Schools* by Mark Prever (2006). Paul Chapman Publishing

■ difficulty in maintaining body heat and often feeling cold

■ distorted body image; fear of being fat when the evidence is to the contrary

■ depression.

How are eating disorders treated?

Eating disorders can be treated by 'talking therapies' such as counselling or psychotherapy. Medication may be prescribed if there are associated problems such as depression or anxiety. Doctors may also offer medical treatment to deal with any of the physical consequences of the eating disorder. Nutritional counselling can support the young person in achieving normal eating patterns as part of the recovery process. In some cases, family work may be suggested to address issues within the family, or self-help groups to prevent isolation and to facilitate mutual support. Serious eating disorders may result in hospitalisation in order to initiate weight gain to prevent death from malnutrition or suicide.

How can the school help?

■ Understand more about these conditions — their causes, symptoms and treatment.

■ Recognise how powerful emotions are for a young person suffering from an eating disorder; these may include shame, guilt, self-disgust or a sense that life is out of control.

■ Be vigilant for the signs of eating distress and be prepared to refer students on. Early intervention is crucial to full recovery.

■ Support the young person emotionally and practically beyond the referral to health specialists.

■ Use PSE/citizenship time to explore the social, cultural and emotional factors associated with food and eating. Be aware of the influence of the media, which emphasise unrealistic images of beauty and physical attractiveness.

■ Become a 'healthy school', promoting healthy eating and exercise.

■ Look beyond the diagnosis and connect with pupils and their distress.

■ Be aware of the values and attitudes promoted by the school, which might be contributing to the problem, as in attitudes toward health and fitness.

■ Offer genuine caring and non-judgemental listening.

■ Be prepared to act as an advocate.

■ Intervene early where there is bullying and teasing about weight and appearance.

■ Build self-esteem.

■ Be patient: eating disorders affect school work and relationships.

■ Ask pupils what help they would like.

P *Mental Health in Schools* by Mark Prever (2006). Paul Chapman Publishing

Obsessive-compulsive disorder

Young people with OCD are plagued by recurring and unwanted thoughts (obsessions) or the need to perform repetitive, ritualistic behaviours (compulsions) that dominate their life and normal functioning. Young people with OCD are aware that their thoughts and behaviours are irrational but may have only fleeting control over them. Rituals such as excessive washing, cleaning, checking, touching and ordering are performed in an attempt to bring relief from obsessive thoughts about dirt, germs and infestation; the fear of committing a violent act; sexual or blasphemous thoughts likely to provoke retribution from a higher being; or anxiety about lack of orderliness, exactness or symmetry. Rituals often bring only temporary respite from the pain and frustration, and when they are not performed, anxiety may rise to unbearable levels. OCD most often begins in childhood and will present itself in a variety of forms and degrees in every secondary school.

Post-traumatic stress disorder (PTSD)

PTSD results from a young person's exposure, either directly or indirectly, to an exceptional or catastrophic event or situation that involved actual or threatened serious injury or death, including murder, rape, domestic violence, car accidents, terrorism, violent street crime, suicide or abuse. There may also have been the direct experience of natural disasters such as floods or tornadoes. For young people coming from abroad, the trauma may have been caused by war or torture. PTSD can have devastating effects on the mental health of a young person. Recurrent and intrusive memories and images of what happened and the fear of its recurence can cause extreme psychological distress. Relationships may become disturbed as emotions are thrown into disarray. Attempts to avoid the feelings and thoughts linked with the trauma may well disrupt life, and anxiety and depression may soon become evident. Hyperarousal, in other words, the constant sense of being under threat, will affect peace of mind and concentration and lead to angry or explosive outbursts. All these symptoms will affect the pupil at home and at school. If left untreated, they may develop into more serious psychiatric illness.

Schizophrenia

Schizophrenia is a serious and complex mental illness largely affecting adults and rare in children. However, a very small number of children, perhaps one or two in every 10,000, may be affected, and such adult psychotic illness may begin to manifest itself in a child as young as seven years of age. The symptoms of childhood and adolescent schizophrenia are similar to those in adults, and include social withdrawal, unnatural and irrational fears, and suspicion of others – for example, patients believe that they are being watched or that people are plotting against them (paranoia). The pupil may have difficulty separating fantasy from reality and might experience sensations such as the voices of people who are not present (hallucinations). They may hold a series of false beliefs; for example, they believe that they have been visited by aliens (delusions). Other characteristics of schizophrenia include odd or eccentric behaviour, such as laughing at sad happenings; disordered or disorganised speech resulting in incoherence; impaired memory; poor social skills; and flat affect, showing little or no emotion and showing little body language or facial expression. Behaviours can include sudden and unpredictable aggression, and catatonic behaviours, such as staring and becoming motionless. Schizophrenia is a difficult mental illness to treat and will inevitably cause not only distress and unhappiness to the young person but much heartbreak and anguish to those around them.

School refusal

What is it?

In school refusal, a pupil does not want to go to school or refuses to do so. In some cases, the young person is brought to school but refuses to stay there. This is very distressing for the pupil's parents and family as well as being a difficult time for children and their school. In my experience, school refusal is a growing problem. School refusal as a description is preferred to the idea of *school phobia*, because school refusal is often caused by a number of problems, some not directly related to school, and it would not meet the criteria usually used to describe *phobia*. School refusal most often occurs at transitions, such as between junior and secondary school, and at times of stress, such as exam periods. Sometimes it begins after a prolonged period of legitimate absence such as during illness. Pupils may suffer from anxiety about attending school for a number of family reasons, including arguments at home and fears that parents may split up, and separation anxiety, especially where there is an overprotective parenting style or where the young person fears for the parent's welfare or health. School-related causes include fear of a particular teacher, dislike of changing for PE, being picked on by older pupils or their peers, having learning difficulties and experiences of failure, and not having friends. Young people will be reluctant to attend school if they perceive it to be unstructured, chaotic and, consequently, unsafe. Boys and girls are affected equally – 1–5% of the school population. School refusal is different from truancy because often the child stays at home and becomes emotionally distressed, and the parent is usually aware of the problem. Truancy mostly involves an attempt to hide non-attendance at school. (See photocopiable pages 61–2)

Self-harm

Deliberate self-harm, also known as *self-injury*, *self-inflicted violence* or *self-mutilation*, is one of the more distressing mental health problems encountered by adults in school. *The Times Educational Supplement* (18 March 2005) records that the national inquiry into self-harm found that 10% of young people aged 15–16 years have deliberately hurt themselves, and that as many as 24,000 under-18s are treated in casualty departments for self-harm each year. Traditionally, self-harm has been seen as injuring oneself by cutting wtih blades, glass or other sharp objects; burning with direct flame, a hot object or chemicals such as aerosols; scratching or rubbing the skin until it bleeds; punching oneself or hard objects; picking at wounds, spots or skin blemishes; and pulling one's own hair. However, taking overdoses, abusing drugs, self-starvation through excessive dieting, and abusing drugs may also be seen as kinds of self-harm. In extreme situations, self-harm may involve taking poisons, jumping in front of cars and jumping from buildings. Considerably more girls self-harm than boys. (See photocopiable pages 63–4)

Photocopiable

How does school refusal show itself?

Pupils may:

- be fearful, overly anxious and distressed at the thought of going to school or whilst there

- display physical symptoms associated with anxiety, such as sweating, increased heartbeat, palpitations or panic attacks

- have recurring headaches

- complain of stomach-ache or nausea

- cry a lot, sometimes in quite distressing ways

- display temper when told they have to go to school

- have problems with sleep and eating patterns

- be clingy and insecure at home

- become markedly less anxious when told they do not have to go to school

- fail to respond to rewards and encouragement to attend school, threats and consequences having equally minimal effect

- threaten to harm themselves if forced to go to school

- become depressed.

How is it treated?

It is important for a doctor to rule out all possible medical causes for non-attendance. The best interventions are often those that are multidisciplinary, involving a number of different professionals. School refusal may coexist with related psychological problems such as depression and anxiety, and these may be treated with a combination of psychiatric drugs and or psychotherapy. It would be unusual for medication to be used to deal with school refusal exclusively. Behavioural interventions may be introduced, such as training in relaxation techniques, assertiveness and social skills. In some cases, approaches such as systematic desensitisation may be tried. This involves gradually exposing young persons to school, in stages, hopefully convincing them that they have nothing to fear. Sometimes family work may be the most productive intervention.

How can the school help?

- Early intervention is crucial. Be prepared to involve an educational psychologist and education social worker at an early stage. A referral to the pupil's GP may result in the involvement of Child and Adolescent Mental Health Services (CAMHS).

P *Mental Health in Schools* by Mark Prever (2006). Paul Chapman Publishing

■ Look for underlying causes; anxiety about attending school may be masking other fears such as fear of being away from a caring parent.

■ Talk with pupils, at home if necessary, asking them to write down their feelings about school. Help them to express their anxieties and concerns. Show that you understand.

■ Work closely with parents and carers, possibly setting up positive reinforcement schemes or asking parents to supervise children on their way to school.

■ Offer pupils reassurance and acknowledge just how difficult it is for them to attend school.

■ Be consistent and firm, avoiding unnecessary changes to your expectations of the young person.

■ Empower pupils and help them to make changes. Encourage them to develop strategies to solve their problem.

■ Involve other pupils; they may be prepared to offer friendship, security and support.

P *Mental Health in Schools* by Mark Prever (2006). Paul Chapman Publishing

Photocopiable

Why do young people self-harm?

The reasons why young people self-harm are usually complex and deep-rooted but probably involve inability to express difficult or distressing feelings in less harmful ways. Self-harm may be seen as an escape from unpleasant emotions such as anger, loss, guilt and shame, and as a way to maintain control over life. It may also represent a form of self-punishment. Some young people report that it helps relieve feelings of numbness and depersonalisation. It has been argued that self-harm is a coping mechanism that lessens the desire to commit suicide, although counter to this is the observation that in some situations deliberate self-harm has led to death when this was not the original intention. Young people sometimes go to great lengths to cover their injuries, especially with clothes. They may also regularly give ordinary reasons for extraordinary injuries. Self-injury can result in infection, scarring and permanent disfigurement.

How is it treated?

Counselling and psychotherapy may be offered alongside drug treatments where there are associated mental health problems such as depression and anxiety. Sometimes a GP will make a referral to CAMHS, and psychiatrists and specialist nurses may become involved. Joining a support or therapeutic group may be recommended. Sometimes creative art therapies can help. Hospitalisation may be a last resort.

How can the school help?

- Make time to listen to the pupil and try to understand.

- Try to connect with the young person behind the self-harm or injury.

- Look for the physical and emotional signs of self-harm and find a sensitive way of initiating a conversation.

- Avoid being judgemental. Do not look shocked, upset, disgusted or anxious, despite how you may be feeling.

- Recognise that self-harm is rarely attention seeking or an attempt to manipulate others. Often it remains hidden.

- Ensure that school personnel receive training.

- Use the school curriculum to explore many of the issues surrounding self-harm in ways that help young people understand self-harm and what causes it, and suggest ways in which they can cope in more positive, less self-destructive ways.

- Build a school community which is caring, supportive and open, and which makes it less likely that a young person will self-harm when faced with difficult feelings.

- Encourage pupils to tell an adult if they know that a pupil in school is self-harming.

© **British Association for Counselling and Psychotherapy 2006 (BACP)**

P *Mental Health in Schools* by Mark Prever (2006). Paul Chapman Publishing

■ Seek out support if you are affected by what you have seen and heard.

■ Understand that self-harm offers young persons a way of coping and that they may be terrified of giving up harming themselves. They may need time to cope in a less harmful way.

■ Be prepared to make a referral to obtain specialist help for the pupil. Where immediate life-saving action is needed, act promptly and call for an ambulance.

■ Do not exclude pupils; they are probably safer at school.

P *Mental Health in Schools* by Mark Prever (2006). Paul Chapman Publishing

Suicide and attempted suicide

A variety of statistics can be found about suicide among young people, but what is clear is that it represents a serious and growing problem. It has been suggested that the estimated suicide rate among young people is higher than the figures published, as some deaths are attributed to other causes such as accidents. Many schools have experienced a suicide attempt or what might be referred to as *parasuicide*, which is a form of self-harm that appears to threaten life but in which victims do not intend actually to kill themselves. Such parasuicide might be seen as a form of communication – an expression of despair and hopelessness. The victims may feel that these acts are the only way of telling others how they really feel.

Suicide is the third leading cause of death in young people, after illness and accidents. Girls attempt suicide more often than boys, but young men are often more successful in completing the task. Whilst figures for adults have remained static, the suicide rate among young people continues to rise. In addition to those who commit or attempt suicide, a number of surveys and my own experience of working with young people suggest that a high proportion of teenagers have considered or had ideas about taking their own life.

There are very few more tragic events than the death of a child by their own hand, and it can have profound and distressing effects on loved ones and the young person's school. Suicide among young people can be avoided by effective prevention, early recognition and treatment, and the secondary school can play a role in all three areas. (See photocopiable pages 66-8)

Photocopiable

Suicide: warning signs

- recognisable and significant mood changes

- unexplained changes in personality

- social withdrawal, especially from friends and family

- deep and apparently unending depression

- changes in weight, eating behaviours, sleep patterns or interest in personal appearance

- low self-esteem

- giving away personal and prized possessions

- loss of interest in life, low levels of motivation, and tiredness and fatigue

- talking about wanting to die or saying that they or other people would be better off if they were dead

- saying that they would not be missed if they were gone

- turning to the misuse of drugs and alcohol (Drugs can be both an indicator and risk factor in the sense that their use may reduce impulse control, or heighten or depress emotions.)

- behavioural changes including uncharacteristic anger and aggression toward peers and adults

- preoccupation with death and dying

- a marked and sudden decline in performance and achievement at school

- gathering information about suicide and its methods

- expression of deep feelings such as despair, hopelessness, shame, guilt, grief, anger and emptiness

- themes of death and sadness in writing, poetry and art, and in the selection of reading material or illustrations

- intentional self-harm such as cutting

- verbalising suicide intent

- previous suicide attempts

- sudden recovery from depression – possibly indicating that a peace has been found with the young person's decision to commit suicide

- current issues of loss in the young person's life through, for example, the death of a parent, divorce, or someone significant to the pupil committing suicide.

P *Mental Health in Schools* by Mark Prever (2006). Paul Chapman Publishing

How is it treated?

If surrounded by secure family and peer relationships, young persons may be offered only brief interventions. However, if young persons have communicated a serious intent to take their own life, or if appropriate support is lacking and there is associated mental illness, the young persons may be hospitalised after a comprehensive assessment. It has been argued frequently that young people who arrive in casualty after a suicide attempt are sometimes treated unsympathetically by doctors. This may have once been the case, but government-initiated guidance has attempted to change attitudes in this area of care. Many of the feelings associated with suicide ideation are linked with depression and are thus treatable with appropriate interventions such as counselling and medication.

How schools can help

- ■ Treat the pupil's problems with care and treat all suicide threats as serious; no talk of suicide should be dismissed as attention seeking or taken lightly. Suicidal verbalisation and 'minor' suicide attempts such as taking a small number of painkillers often precede more serious attempts.

- ■ Train staff to detect the signs of depression and potential suicide, and be prepared to make immediate and appropriate referrals to social services and health professionals, such as the school nurse or GP. If in doubt, seek professional advice.

- ■ Suicide-prevention programmes remain controversial, some people believing that they may increase risk. However, a comprehensive approach to emotional literacy may enable young people to learn the vocabulary and skills to express difficult and deep-rooted feelings. Schools may also teach problem-solving skills.

- ■ Be aware of individual students at risk due to particular circumstances; at-risk groups such as pregnant schoolgirls, gifted and talented young people, and children with a family history of suicide; and complicating mental health issues affecting children or their family.

- ■ Notice when a pupil appears to be low or sad.

- ■ Offer non-judgemental listening, but no single adult in the school should be supporting a depressed pupil alone.

- ■ Listen to the pupil's words, but also to what is being communicated covertly. Listen also to what is not being said: does the young person fail to express a sense of future?

- ■ The school should have a named individual, known to staff, that will receive and respond to concerns.

- ■ Where an adult is supporting an unhappy pupil, remember to let the pupil know that there are limits to the confidentiality a school can offer.

P *Mental Health in Schools* **by Mark Prever (2006). Paul Chapman Publishing**

■ The school should not wait for a crisis but intervene early, supporting pupils who have experienced a difficult event or period in their lives before more acute behaviours begin to cause concern.

■ If a referral has been made and the pupil remains in school, continue to offer support and to work closely with other agencies involved.

■ Build self-esteem.

Intervention with a suicidal pupil

■ If suicide has been attempted, offer appropriate first aid and seek immediate medical attention.

■ Calm the situation and avoid the involvement of too many adults. Where appropriate, a close friend of the pupil can be encouraged to offer support. If possible, remove the young person to a quiet place and encourage talking. Be prepared for silence and be patient.

■ Encourage the pupil to give up any dangerous objects or medications, but do not use force.

■ Observe the pupil whilst talking. Listen intently and reflect back how the young person is feeling.

■ Avoid interrogation and intrusive questioning.

■ Contact parents or carers. Seek advice from social services and health professionals.

P *Mental Health in Schools* by Mark Prever (2006). Paul Chapman Publishing

Reflection box

◆ Mental health issues affect us all, directly or indirectly. As you read this chapter, which of the problems described could you identify with for personal reasons? Which affected you emotionally? Did you recognise any aspects of yourself?

◆ Which kinds of mental illness do you have most 'sympathy' with. What moral, political or ethical questions were raised for you?

◆ Which mental health problems were you most informed about? Which do you need to understand more?

◆ How sensitive is your school to the kinds of problems described here?

◆ Which 'signs and symptoms' or specific mental health problems could most easily be missed or misinterpreted, leading to inappropriate behavioural interventions?

CHAPTER 6

A whole-school and multiagency approach

This chapter will show:

The emotional side of school often remains hidden, yet it has powerful influences on all that happens there. Mental health is best addressed by a whole-school approach, and this can be achieved in quite creative ways. Key to a whole-school approach is the issue of addressing stigma, which can have debilitating effects. Working closely with outside agencies is crucial if we are to ensure effective prevention, early intervention and support for young people with mental health problems in our schools.

Schools are emotional places

Schools are infinitely emotional places, yet this dimension to schooling is sometimes not recognised. Imagine for a moment an average secondary school of around 1000 pupils with over 100 teaching and non-teaching staff. Each person enters that school daily, infused with a multitude of emotions, multiplied and compounded by the process of teaching and learning, and the relationships that underpin this endeavour. Thoughts, feelings and behaviours ricochet like a pinball machine, forming almost infinite permutations. Among those 1000 pupils, adolescent hormones pump around the body causing frustration, anger and confusion. Questions about identity and sexuality abound. If we take all this into account, it is hardly surprising that things happen in school: pupils fight or feel themselves attracted to each other; teachers shout, become upset or work in fear of someone seeing that they cannot cope; friendships emerge but then fail, leaving winners and losers; pupils exert power over others, who fall victim. The list is endless and remarkably complex. In the light of the above, I sometimes question the whole idea of schooling; the idea of 1100 or more people in a cauldron of emotion trying to teach and learn makes schools seem an odd invention!

Of course, it has been increasingly documented that emotions affect learning. In a positive sense, we remember best when what we learn has an emotional context – when what we are asked to retain or learn to do is infused with personal meaning. The key moments I can recollect from my school days are those associated with fear, pride, disappointment, excitement, shame and a sense of being part of something.

Undoubtedly, too, difficult emotions and raw feelings can act as a barrier to learning. A pupil who is stressed because of home conflict may find it hard to focus on algebra; a young person grieving for a loved grandparent may find it difficult to concentrate on Henry VIII; a child deep in depression may find it hard to find the energy to participate in games or other physical activity. A child who has problems with establishing a normal eating pattern may think primarily of food and weight, and the pupil who is terrified of being in school may think only of going home.

Experience tells me that motivation is the prime mover in achievement, and it is most energised when pupils have a sense of future and direction, and least evident where they strive hopelessly to find meaning. I believe that no young person sets out to fail, but some behave in a way that suggests they do not care.

As professionals in schools, we sometimes are unaware of, or less tuned in to, the emotional dimension and, in particular, our own feelings. We, too, may be having difficulties in our own lives, which inevitably affect our performance and relationships. Sometimes professionals in school see pupils primarily as learners in a narrow sense, and the increasing focus on teaching and learning often recognises how our brains work but says little about the part emotions play. Learning is never an emotionally neutral experience, and it will serve to enhance or diminish self-esteem. Pupils develop a whole range of defences to defend vigorously their fragile self-esteem. As adults, we are no different.

A mentally healthy school recognises this parallel dimension and its impact. A school that is sensitive to the emotional needs of young people and which places mental health at the core of its aims is likely to be more successful than that which has identified achievement in narrow academic terms. Such a school seeks to promote healthy minds whilst at the same time being aware of the role the school can play in supporting those with emerging difficulties. It is also aware of its capacity to contribute to or exacerbate the kinds of mental health problems that young people carry through the school gates with their school bags.

A whole-school approach to mental health

Whilst it is hoped that the home and family are the prime source of nurturing and support, it is recognised that this may not always be the case. Schools, too, may contribute to the stress and unhappiness in a young person's life, but they can also be places of growth where mental health is promoted and young people supported. Young people spend significant amounts of time in school, and this can make a real difference to their current and future lives. It is recognised that this can truly be achieved only by a whole-school approach.

A whole-school approach to mental health will not simply happen – any more than a language or science curriculum will be delivered by chance. It needs to be thought out and planned for. A mentally healthy school does not delve into the emotional world of young people in some token way that allows boxes to be ticked on school self-evaluation forms. It takes mental health matters seriously, possibly seeing them as the most important factor in school success, underpinning everything else that happens within its walls and beyond.

Mental health is seen as all-encompassing and operating on many fronts simultaneously, and not confined to a single dimension. The school places mental health and emotional well-being at the forefront of its thinking and central to its aims. This all-embracing aspect of school is seen as connected, and not fragmented, and each aspect of school life is both affected and influenced by its ideas and philosophy. Mental health is made explicit, not hidden, and is high on the agenda of change and development. It is seen as being part of long-term development, and is not short term or transitory. It needs to be sustainable and not likely to fade. A mental health approach ensures that it is resilient and not cast aside by future centrally enforced initiatives, but has a word to say on their introduction.

Mental health should permeate all aspects of school life and learning. Everybody is involved regardless of role or status. Mental health should be seen as everyone's business, and not confined to school-based specialists or merely the concern of outside agencies and mental health professionals. Mental health affects our approach to the curriculum; it is there in every relationship and every interaction between adult and child. Mental health is part of teaching and learning, in leadership and management at all levels from classroom to senior leadership team. Mental health should be there in our staff development programmes, sometimes explicitly and sometimes simply as a perspective. It should be identifiable in school policy and most importantly in our pastoral care systems and relationships with parents and carers.

Mental health in a secondary school may be seen as operating on three levels. The first is concerned with school ethos, climate, organisation and curriculum. This is about our school environment and its capacity to promote and support – or undermine – mental health. This level is about prevention and awareness. The second level is concerned with early intervention, seeking to reduce risk and increase resilience. The third stage represents the school's capacity to respond swiftly and intelligently to expressed need. This level is concerned with the school's ability to offer individualised and intensive support, and also recognise when referral to other agencies and professionals is needed.

Perhaps most significant in mental health is a concern for the culture and climate of the school. These are difficult concepts to define but are of profound importance. Anyone entering a secondary school will soon get a feel for it. A positive school climate will be seen in the faces of the young people and the adults who work there. A mentally healthy school would seek to uphold and pass on to others a variety of beliefs, values, norms and shared traditions that promote a feeling of caring, collegiality, cooperation, connectedness, inclusion and belonging. Relationships would show evidence of mutual respect, trust, warmth and openness. This will be there in the type of language used between all adults and young people and in the friendships that emerge. It would also be there in how men and women and boys and girls relate to each other, and in the friendships that form between young people of different faiths, beliefs and ethnicity. In contrast, a negative school culture is characterised by power, exclusion, conflict, separateness and harassment.

It is not possible to state how important it is to recognise the role schools play in the promotion of mental health. Some argue that mental health is not the concern of schools. In response, it must be said that mental health is *already* happening in our schools, regardless of preference and beliefs about the purpose of education. The task of the school is to ensure that this is a positive, comprehensive and coherent process.

What can schools do to promote mental health and support young people?

Good schools will already be health-promoting schools, and many of the ideas set out below simply represent good practice. However, it is worth highlighting some of these to enable schools to evaluate themselves and focus some of their energies in this direction. The ideas below will contribute to some understanding as to what might constitute a mentally healthy school.

Photocopiable

The mentally healthy school

Ethos and organisation

- Work to create a school environment in which pupils feel psychologically safe and secure. This should be a priority in line with the government papers, **Healthy Schools and Every Child Matters**.

- Foster a sense of belonging, as by the use of first names or welcoming pupils into school and classroom. The need to belong goes back to the child in all of us.

- Regard each young person as of equal status. This aim is easily stated but difficult to deliver. This means valuing those students who are not likely to contribute to measurable outcomes and may themselves appear to be a drain on time and resources.

- Help pupils adapt to change and establish routines around school and classroom. Provide consistency and continuity. Young people can react negatively to change, and this can result in stress and anxiety.

- Be a school which challenges the stigma of mental illness and teaches tolerance and understanding. Display posters, include stigma in the curriculum and address it in assembly.

- Locate a whole-school approach to mental health in the context of a wider concern for the creation of a healthy school. This may include associated areas such as healthy eating and fitness.

- Give pupils a voice, as through a school council. This will offset disaffection and alienation and give pupils a sense of power to effect change. A school council also provides a listening device, enabling the school to gain a sense of what school is really like for the pupils who attend there.

- Respect confidentiality. Have clear policies on who can share what information with whom. Make clear the limits to confidentiality from the start.

- Ensure that the school has a clear, fair and consistent behaviour policy. Young people thrive best when they know where boundaries are, and when they feel safe from physical or psychological harm. Poor discipline increases stress and is an additional risk factor, especially if young people are already experiencing problems in their lives.

- Deal quickly and effectively with racial, sexual and other forms of harassment. Ensure the school has comprehensive and well-documented policies in these areas.

- Make school interesting and stimulating. Work hard to prevent boredom and disengagement.

- Make school a safe place in which pupils can talk about feelings.

© British Association for Counselling and Psychotherapy 2006 (BACP)

P *Mental Health in Schools* by Mark Prever (2006). Paul Chapman Publishing

Awareness

- Increase staff awareness and understanding of mental health issues through training and experience. The school should be prepared to include mental health as part of its professional development programme. Many of the major organisations listed at the end of this book hold conferences and training events, and some will train staff within the school. Many of the generalist training agencies now advertise courses relating to mental health and emotional well-being. Information about specific mental health problems is available on the internet, and specialist organisations often produce excellent materials for professionals.

- Understand the tasks of adolescence that need to be negotiated, and build this awareness into your ideas and practice.

- Recognise that you are working with young and developing minds; handle with care.

- Look at your own lifestyle and way of being. Be a positive role model.

- Be aware of the effect of school on your own emotional health. Look after yourself.

- Understand the importance of good mental health in the adults who work in school. Ensure that staff are equally supported and valued.

Relationships

- Watch what we say. Our words can be powerful and can build up young people or undermine their confidence and sense of self.

- Show patience. Adolescence is a time of challenge, independence and search for identity.

- Accentuate the positive. Encourage and support but do not attempt to coerce pupils into feeling good. They may need to feel sad for a while.

- Build on young people's strengths and qualities.

- Like adults, young people develop a range of defences. These may be necessary for survival. Understand that a pupil's behaviour or attitude may not be about you at all.

- Treat pupils as young adults in the making, but offer and expect respect.

- Build the kinds of relationships with young people that make for self-esteem and increase resilience.

- Find ways to help young people relate and learn the skills of friendship.

- Be sensitive to anger and frustration. Accept that anger is OK as long as the angry young persons do not hurt themselves, other people or property. Encourage pupils to express their anger in meaningful ways that communicate without destroying relationships.

P   *Mental Health in Schools* by Mark Prever (2006). Paul Chapman Publishing

Curriculum

■ Promote emotional literacy. In particular, help pupils develop a sophisticated emotional vocabulary.

■ All subjects contribute to the social and emotional development of pupils and mental health — through both content and the process of teaching and learning.

■ Look closely at teaching and learning in the school. Recognise that we all learn in different ways.

■ Ensure that the school offers mental health resources of all kinds and make these readily available to parents and particularly young people.

■ Develop an extensive programme of extra-curricular activity and encourage the positive use of leisure time.

■ Teach about mental health issues, such as bereavement and loss; be prepared to address controversial and sensitive issues openly and honestly. Many of the organisations listed in Chapter 9, 'Useful Organisations and Resources', provide materials for young people that can be incorporated into the school's PSE programme. Some have published specific teaching packs for use in school. A number of companies produce catalogues of materials relating to key areas such as bullying, bereavement, self-esteem and working with emotions. A number of these are listed in the useful website section of Chapter 9.

■ Be concerned about failure and its devastating impact on young, impressionable minds.

Intervention

■ Encourage staff to be observant, noticing those little changes in personality and behaviour that might indicate that something is wrong, thereby facilitating early intervention. This is about sensitivity and awareness amid the stress and activity of school life.

■ Teachers are not mental health professionals. We should not simply 'double up' as psychologists, doctors or nurses but be clear about the part schools can play in mental health promotion, prevention and intervention.

■ Recognise the school's limitations and establish clear lines of referral.

■ Have systems in place to track vulnerable pupils, ensuring that no pupil is overlooked or gets lost in the system.

■ Do not be a school that reacts. Be proactive and anticipate problems.

■ Consider the appointment or designation of a mental health coordinator in the school – someone who will maintain an essential overview and who can ensure that mental health remains high on the agenda. This is most likely to be a member of the senior leadership team who will also have oversight of **Healthy Schools** and **Every Child Matters**. A really committed school could appoint a professional with a specific responsibility for mental health and emotional well being.

■ Ensure that mental health has an active and secure place in the school's improvement plan.

■ Be a listening school. Whilst there is an important place for advice and guidance, adults should create the time and space to really listen to pupils.

■ Make it acceptable that a pupil can talk with an adult of their choice in school when they feel the need.

■ Have clear policies and procedures for offering help when a pupil experiences the death of a loved one, is self-harming or has experienced trauma. It may also be a good idea to establish a crisis response team.

■ Involve parents and families early and meaningfully as real partners, not just when the problem becomes too deep-rooted or appears insurmountable.

■ Put in place effective procedures for child protection. The school needs to create the kind of relationships and opportunities that make disclosure of abuse more likely. Understand that support continues beyond referral to social services and other agencies.

■ Watch keenly for the silent, hidden, lonely and isolated pupils in your school.

■ Take an active anti-bullying stance. Bullying can have a profound and lasting effect on the psychological well-being of the victim. Have clear policies in place, make the issue high profile, and encourage a clear anti-bullying ethos. LEAs offer written guidance here, as do a number of organisations listed in Chapter 9.

■ An efficient and effective special educational needs department is essential if pupils with social and emotional problems and learning difficulties are to be identified early, and interventions planned and delivered. Unmet special needs will contribute to mental health problems in the school.

■ Establish a place of silence in the school for pupils and adults where they really can experience 'time out'.

■ Make it a priority to develop close working relationships with mental health professionals and those individuals and agencies who may be able to support pupils in distress.

■ Be aware of mental health issues at times of transition, as when pupils transfer from junior school. This is when some young people begin to fail and experience distress.

■ Never give up on a young person. Work to build meaning, hope and a sense of future.

P *Mental Health in Schools* **by Mark Prever (2006). Paul Chapman Publishing**

Combating stigma

Society has always felt uncomfortable with mental illness; indeed, there is a long history of mystery, prejudice, fear and discrimination over many hundreds of years. However, we are now in the early years of a new millennium in which such attitudes and beliefs are no longer acceptable and should be challenged. Ideas about mental health are passed on by our family and friends, but the school is the obvious place to challenge stereotypes and negative attitudes that have an effect on those suffering from mental health problems – and all of us indirectly. Words like 'psycho', 'loony', 'schizo', 'crazy', 'nuts', 'insane' and 'mad' are used frequently by adults and children alike. The media influence us in significant ways, mentally ill people being portrayed as unattractive, violent, dangerous, unpredictable, needing to be restrained by straitjackets, and even as killers. In particular, newspapers are keen to highlight the mental health problems of people who commit the most horrendous crimes. Misconceptions about mental illness are also exploited by advertisers to improve sales and promote their clients' products. All this fuels fear and anxiety and can lead to further stereotyping and stigma. We are also exposed to the idea that the mentally ill are there to be made fun of through jokes and humour. Moreover, despite the advances in psychology, medicine and neuroscience over the last decade or so, the mentally ill are portrayed as lazy, inadequate, weak, self-indulgent and incompetent.

Stigma is a sign of shame and disgrace that affects how others perceive you and how you see yourself. By the time pupils start secondary school, they have already been exposed to many of the negative ideas described here, and young, impressionable minds will absorb these to the detriment of themselves and those around them. Mental health problems are not always visible in the way that physical illnesses often are. Mental illness can be referred to as the invisible illness despite associated physiological causes and effects. Many people experience mental health problems, to a lesser or greater degree, at some point in their lives.

It is these ideas which we should also be exposing pupils to in school through the curriculum. A number of published programmes now expect pupils to explore the issue of stigma head on. Clearly, exposing young people to the facts about mental illness is important if stigma is to be eradicated. The Mental Health Awareness in Action project in London saw the charity Rethink and the Institute of Psychiatry set out to address mental health stigma through raising awareness in secondary school students (Pinfold, 2003). Among the concepts and ideas presented were that mental health problems are common and affect everybody, that people can recover from mental illness, that discrimination can seriously affect people with mental health problems, and that any link between mental illness and violent behaviour is a myth. The programme showed that teaching about mental health could reduce stigma but that these ideas needed to be reinforced. One way to do this is to ensure that mental health issues figure prominently in the school curriculum, through both specific subjects and, more discretely, through personal and social education/citizenship lessons. (See photocopiable page 78)

A multiagency approach

There are strong arguments to support the idea that schools should be the focus of child and adolescent mental health provision. As stated earlier, young people spend many of their waking hours in school, and teachers and other school-based professionals have traditionally provided

Photocopiable

The effects of stigma

The stigma of mental illness can affect both adults and young people in a variety of ways. Affected people might:

- experience fear, ridicule and rejection by other people

- not seek help when they need it, for fear of being devalued or labelled

- hide their feelings, suffer in secrecy and disguise their symptoms

- feel inferior and outside the 'group'

- become isolated from friends and family

- develop low self-esteem and diminished confidence

- experience discrimination; as adults, having difficulty with gaining insurance, employment and finance

- feel a deep sense of shame, guilt and hopelessness – possibly leading to self-harm and suicidal behaviour

- not recover from their illness as quickly as expected. People suffering from mental illness often claim that the stigma and the negative attitudes of other people are as distressing as the experience of the mental illness itself.

In establishing a whole-school approach to addressing stigma, it is important that we begin with ourselves as professionals. It is desirable that we:

- increase our knowledge and understanding of mental health and the range of mental illness and its causes

- explore and challenge our own attitudes to mental health and address any stereotypes and misconceptions

- be prepared to challenge comments made by colleagues, parents and pupils

- ensure that the school is not discriminating against pupils and adults who may be experiencing a mental health problem

- encourage young people to seek support when they need it

- do not refer to a pupil as 'depressed' but, rather, as having depression (This applies to all diagnosed mental illnesses.)

- be aware of the mental health issues in our own lives and how we need to be understood and supported at that time.

P *Mental Health in Schools* by Mark Prever (2006). Paul Chapman Publishing

support for pupils with social, emotional and behavioural problems; therefore, this way of working, with education at the core, would seem appropriate. In the United States, school-based mental health is more common and has brought some success. Schools would, I believe, welcome the on-site involvement of mental health professionals – because it is more common now to feel out of their depth with some of the young people they meet. School-based mental health services would also reduce stigma in seeking and accessing mental health services, and make services more widely available. The government paper *Every Child Matters* and subsequent legislation, and the move toward extended schools, will encourage and compel schools and other organisations to work more closely together, and this is to be welcomed.

Interagency collaboration will not come without its problems, and anecdotal evidence suggests that whilst schools are very willing to cooperate, they currently face an inordinate amount of pressure to reach targets and compete with other schools in league tables. Generally, practitioners across all disciplines may feel anxious about interagency collaboration. Each agency working with young people brings its own aims, objectives and ways of working. They will have professionally defined priorities that may also be influenced by local and central government expectations. These differing perspectives will often be found in the different language that is used and the different methodology. Schools may also feel that they cannot deliver what is necessary, as time in school is scarce and initiatives and change abound.

The benefits of multiagency working will include improved communication, earlier intervention, more effective referral routes and procedures, and, hopefully, increased understanding of the roles which professionals play in the wider scheme of things. All this can only benefit young people in difficulty and their parents, who often crave help and support. Multiagency working requires clarity of roles and an understanding of what each agency and professional does. There should be no threat here, as each has a unique contribution to make. A common sense of purpose will not come easily and coordination both within the school and beyond will be necessary – but is not impossible.

In the context of this book, I would encourage schools to widen their thinking and look beyond passive referral to real joint working. The school will need to educate itself about what organisations are doing with young people and how they can link and work together more closely. I am not talking here exclusively about the statutory sector, either. Schools traditionally have been less confident in engaging with the voluntary sector, which has less of an 'official feel' and possibly the image of less accountability, yet my own experience tells me that this is where some of the most committed and targeted work can be found. Attitudes are changing, and voluntary agencies are also equally keen to work in the school setting as previously uncharted territory. It would be a good idea to find out what organisations exist locally and who may be able to provide appropriate services. Most authorities produce directories of this kind. Establish contact and form relationships with specific individuals. Visit and find out what they do and how they can help. However, the best interagency work comes with actual use and working alongside professionals from other professions and disciplines. This can only be a desirable development.

Multiagency working means more than passing on young people to so-called specialists. It has the potential for worthwhile collaboration and sharing of expertise, and fills me with excitement and hope. Schools will need to find the time to make this happen, but the benefits in the long term will be noticeable. Schools are powerful organisations and historically have been less enthusiastic about changes encouraged or facilitated by ■ those outside the sector. Changes in the way government departments themselves cooperate may also be necessary. However, if schools have the desire and will, change can happen and there is significant evidence that the process has begun.

It would seem appropriate at this point to consider how the present child and adolescent mental health services operate and to consider the roles of mental health professionals who might come into contact with schools directly.

Child and Adolescent Mental Health Services (CAMHS)

CAMHS may be seen as a model that sets out and contextualises all the services that promote the mental health and psychological well-being of children and young people.

The CAMHS concept includes all services working with young people in a multiplicity of settings. Some of these are directly concerned with mental health, whilst other more universal services, such as education, are seen as part of the wider picture. This supports the ideas presented in this book, that mental health is the concern of all professionals who work with young people, and is not just the preserve of mental health specialists. There are, of course, different levels of mental health promotion, prevention, early intervention and specialist input, and the CAMHS model recognises these differences within the wider concept of a comprehensive, coordinated approach to the mental health needs of children and young people.

The tiered approach set out briefly below is not a statutory or centrally controlled system. It is best seen as a helpful conceptual framework through which services can be commissioned and needs identified and met most appropriately.

Tier 1

Tier 1 comprises front-line professionals who have little or no specialist mental health knowledge but are often the adults most commonly exposed to young people in difficulty on a daily basis. They include:

- general practitioners (GPs)
- teachers
- generic social workers
- children's residential workers
- youth workers
- school nurses
- health visitors
- youth justice workers
- voluntary agencies
- the police.

These non-specialists are in an excellent position to identify problems as soon as they begin, and make referrals to more specialist services. They are also in a prime position to promote mental health and prevent problems from developing. In some cases, experienced professionals at this level may be in a position to offer advice to young people and their parents about the less severe problems that sometimes present in young people.

Tier 2

Professionals working at tier 2 have some specialist knowledge and experience. They often work in collaboratively with other services at this level but do not usually form part of an identified team. They include:

- clinical child psychologists
- counsellors working in GP practices
- educational psychologists
- community psychiatric nurses
- education welfare officers
- Connexions workers
- psychotherapists
- behaviour support teams
- community paediatricians
- psychiatrists.

Specialists at this level may also operate in tiers 3 or 4. They may be involved in offering training to professionals at tier 1. However, much of their time is spent offering advice and consultation to families and other professionals. They also have a pivotal role to play in the assessment of more complex need that may require intervention at a higher level of expertise.

Tier 3

These professionals are normally working within a coordinated team based in a mental health clinic or through child psychiatric outpatient services. They offer support to children, young people and their families where more severe, complex and persistent mental health problems have been identified. Tier 3 professionals include:

- child and adolescent psychiatrists
- clinical psychologists
- community psychiatric nurses
- child psychotherapists
- occupational therapists

- art, play, music and drama therapists

- specialist social workers.

Tier 4

This tier offers highly specialised interventions for young people with the most advanced, complex and persistent mental illnesses that require considerable specialist knowledge, skills, experience and of course resources. Tier 4 intervention includes in-patient psychiatric units for adolescents, units for those with severe eating disorders, specialist neuropsychiatric teams, specialist facilities for young people with significant sensory disabilities, secure forensic adolescent units and specialist teams working, for example, with victims of trauma and sexual abuse.

Intelligent referral

Achieving the right balance between school-based support and referral to an outside agency can be difficult. In some cases, referral criteria have been clearly established, or at least there is an understanding between the school and other professionals as to when to refer. For example, an education social worker normally becomes involved where there is poor or erratic attendance. Behaviour-support services work with pupils who do not appear to have responded to a range of school-based interventions. A Connexions worker may receive a referral for a pupil who is disaffected and with an uncertain future. Of course, the most clearly defined referrals are those to social services where a young person is deemed to be at risk of physical, emotional or sexual abuse or neglect. Schools have a regulated responsibility to refer such concerns within a short period of disclosure.

However, in my experience, schools either refer too early, before exhausting possible school support, or delay until matters have got out of hand. An 'intelligent' referral is one that attempts to identify the need and referral route. Many exclusion centres are full of pupils experiencing a whole range of emotional problems that have been misinterpreted and left untreated.

It is important to see referral as a process rather than an action taken whereby responsibility for a young person is passed to another agency. Normally, the pupil remains in the school and is entitled to support alongside referral. The young persons need to be involved in this process, as do their parents. The reasons for the referral should be made clear, and an opportunity to discuss feelings about the referral made available. A referral 'imposed' upon a child or family is less likely to be successful, and professionals working in the statutory and voluntary sector become frustrated when a young person appears at the door, at best with little understanding of what is happening and at worst angry and resistant.

Referrals are made when there is concern for a young person's social, emotional or physical well-being, and when intervention is seen to be beyond the expertise of the school. Schools are quite experienced at recognising when a young person's behaviour, thinking or emotions are beyond the norm, causing concern both in school and at home. Most organisations and agencies are more than willing to offer advice and to have a discussion about the young person before a formal referral is made. Mental health referrals are normally made through the child's GP, the school nurse or the school medical officer. Such referrals should be made as early as possible but particularly when the following concerns have been identified.

Photocopiable

Mental health problems: when to refer on

Where there is evidence of:

- persistent and debilitating low mood or depression

- social isolation and withdrawal

- severe anxiety or unnatural fears

- self-harm, particularly self-mutilation

- excessive use of alcohol or drugs

- expression of suicidal thoughts or intent

- the pupil appearing to hallucinate, hear voices, have delusions or be paranoid

- obsessive-compulsive behaviour

- problems with normal eating or purging or dieting excessively

- the young person having significant difficulties in forming and maintaining peer relationships

- pupils expressing concerns about their own emotional health or 'sanity'

- the young person appearing out of control, having persistent anger or violent tendencies or expressing concerns about harming another person

- bizarre or inexplicable behaviour

- the young person appearing stuck in grief or loss

- attachment problems

- developmental difficulties, such as bedwetting, soiling and sleep disturbance

- very low self-esteem

- marked mood swings

- the pupil having experienced significant trauma, which appears to be affecting thoughts, feelings and behaviour

- the pupil appearing unable to function on a day-to-day basis.

Clearly, it is difficult in a book of this kind to be more specific about when to refer. Each child is an individual with complex needs and circumstances. Intelligent referral comes from knowing the pupil thoroughly and when the school can show that normal interventions have failed. It is important to speak to colleagues in supporting professions and seek their advice. If a young person's mood and behaviour change rapidly or in

P *Mental Health in Schools* by Mark Prever (2006). Paul Chapman Publishing

unusual ways, or if they become a danger to themselves or others, particularly if there is evidence of self-harm or suicidal thoughts or actions, a referral should be made as soon as possible.

Making a referral

When one makes a referral, it is always useful to have the following kinds of information available:

- full name of the pupil being referred

- address, including postcode

- date of birth

- parent/carer's name and contact numbers, especially if these are different from the child's

- known siblings, including those currently at the school

- an up-to-date printout of the pupil's attendance

- why the young person is being referred

- any familial history that may be relevant

- school history including behaviour and achievement levels

- a record of school-based interventions

- any special educational needs

- involvement of other agencies

- details of any child-protection or social services involvement.

P *Mental Health in Schools* by Mark Prever (2006). Paul Chapman Publishing

Reflection box

◆ What can you remember about school? Can you identify the emotional context of your recollections?

◆ Look back at the section on ways in which schools can promote mental health and support young people. Use it as a kind of audit tool. What is your school already doing and what needs more attention?

◆ How would you describe the 'climate' of your school?

◆ What attitudes to mental illness exist among pupils and staff in your school?

◆ What agencies is your school already working with?

◆ Consider the different emphasis, focus and language of each of the mental health agencies and professionals mentioned in this chapter. How do these compare with your school's focus and objectives?

The mental health curriculum: resources for use with pupils

This chapter looks at:

Issues around mental health should be raised with pupils directly through the taught curriculum. This serves to raise awareness, increase knowledge, improve skills and reduce stigma. The following classroom materials are designed for use during PSHE time or for small group use.

Mental health is promoted through the ethos of the schools and should be enshrined in the relationships, policies and procedures that exist there. However, mental health issues should also form part of the curriculum. A number of subjects will, by their very nature, explore matters relating to feelings and matters of life and death. Indeed, it could be argued that every subject on the school curriculum in some way contributes to this aspect of the development of our pupils.

It is my belief that, through the PSE/citizenship curriculum, topics of direct importance to mental health should be introduced, despite sometimes being controversial or of a sensitive nature. Mental health problems are a reality for many of our pupils, directly or indirectly, and to shy away from them is to deny young people the opportunity to explore these matters in ways that help them deal with them if and when they happen.

The following resource materials are drawn from a BACP publication, *Exploring Mental Health: A Teaching Resource for Schools – for Work With Students Aged 14–16* (Prever, 2004). The resource is for whole-class use but can be adapted for small groups. Having used these materials with older pupils and even adults, I believe that they can be used beyond the originally stated 16-year limit, which was always an arbitrary line dictated to some extent by the school curriculum. It is the quality of the discussion which differentiates between ages and offers a potential resource for use with older pupils.

A note of caution is necessary. In using these materials, we must recognise that some of the issues and ideas may well touch some of our pupils more than others. It is important to check at the end of each session that pupils are feeling OK, and that support structures are in place to help pupils who have been affected by content and discussion. The teacher should also ensure that they have a colleague with whom to share strong feelings if necessary. This resource should be used sensitively and with empathy. Please note that some activity pages are photocopiable for class use.

1. Words, stereotypes and feelings

Activity guidance notes for teachers

These activities ask pupils to explore the language of mental health and the attitudes linked to it. Pupils are also encouraged to look at stereotypes associated with mental health and to challenge these. Finally, pupils are asked to consider their own feelings and those of others in relation to the language explored.

Time

50 minutes.

What you will need

- large sheets of paper
- felt-tip pens.

How to do it

Split the pupils into groups of four. Hand them the pens and paper and ask them to carry out a wordstorm around the idea of *mental health*. Remember, at this stage, all contributions are welcomed and not challenged. After five minutes, ask each group to display their results and share with the whole group. Often the list of words will focus on mental *illness* and include a number of slang words that are often seen as offensive or ill-informed, such as *nutter, dimwit, mad, schizo, not all there, odd, crazy* or *loony*. How many words are seen to be positive or negative? Ask the pupils if they have ever used words like these. What feelings are generated in the person who uses these words: fear, superiority, separateness?

Explore with the group the possible origin of some of these words and the possible effect upon our attitudes to people with mental health problems. What might they feel: isolation, shame, anxiety, not belonging, inferiority, anger? Raise the idea that mental *health* is also about being emotionally healthy and not exclusively about illness. Assess with the group the possible impact on people with mental health problems, especially in terms of their sense of worth and relationships.

Give out more paper. Now, ask the pupils, working with a partner, to draw the outline figure of a 'mentally ill person'. They should then label their visual representation. Allow ten minutes for this. Ask them to share with another pair and look for similarities. Clearly, some pupils may resist creating the stereotype but encourage them to do so if only to highlight the attitudes that persist in society.

Extension activities

Ask the group to think of how mental health is portrayed in film and on television. Are these stereotypes?

---

2. Myth and reality

Activity guidance notes for teachers

There are many myths associated with mental illness, which have been adopted almost as unquestionable truths. These activities encourage discussion around attitudes and knowledge.

Time

35 minutes.

✎ What you will need

- a copy of the activity sheet, 'Mental Illness: True or False' (included in this chapter) for each pupil

- two sheets of A4 paper, one labelled TRUE and the other FALSE

- Pens for pupils.

How to do it

Ask the pupils to complete the activity sheet 'Mental Illness: True or False'. This should be done by gut feeling rather than extensive deliberation. Allow five minutes for this before asking pupils to pair up and compare responses. To what extent is there agreement? Where there is disagreement, each pupil should try to explain the reasoning behind their choice. The following information is reproduced for your use:

1. Only a very small proportion of people with mental illness are in danger of harming others. Mental illness is more often associated with withdrawal and silent suffering.

2. Mental health problems rarely affect intelligence. Some patients have lower levels of intelligence and some are above average.

3. Mental health problems affect many people either directly or indirectly throughout their lives. Whilst most people do not suffer from a psychotic illness, many people are affected by neurotic symptoms. Mental health problems affect people regardless of race, religion, nationality or gender.

4. Children experience mental health problems, although these are often not diagnosed or treated.

5. Self-harm is most often a secretive activity and a form of coping.

6. Many illnesses can be treated and managed, and often people will return to normal functioning, but people with severe mental illness sometimes experience difficulties throughout their lives.

7. Depression has nothing to do with being weak or lazy and is sometimes associated with changes in brain chemistry. The causes of depression are complex, and whilst all people have to take some responsibility for their thoughts, feelings and behaviour, depression is not a choice, and we should not apportion blame or withhold support.

8. Mental illness, while affecting other people around the sufferer, is not contagious.

9. 'Mental illness' is a generic term that refers primarily to a group of illnesses of the mind, in the same way that heart disease refers to a range of illnesses of the heart and circulatory system.

10. Some tendencies to mental illness may be passed on between generations biologically, and whilst poor parenting may be a significant risk factor, it is unlikely to be the sole cause of severe mental illness.

Extension activities

As an alternative to pair work, consider placing your two TRUE/FALSE sheets at opposite ends of the room and, on reading the statement, ask pupils to move to the side which represents their opinion. They should be prepared to comment on their choice. Where there is a disagreement and different views expressed, invite pupils at opposing ends of the room to change their mind and join the opposite group.

Photocopiable

Activity 2   Activity Sheet – Mental Illness: True or False

Decide which of the following statements are TRUE or FALSE. Circle your answer. Be prepared to discuss your choices.

1. People with a mental illness are dangerous.   **TRUE   FALSE**

2. People suffering from a mental illness are often below average in intelligence.   **TRUE   FALSE**

3. Mental health problems affect most people at some point in their lives.   **TRUE   FALSE**

4. Children do not suffer from mental illness.   **TRUE   FALSE**

5. People who self-harm are seeking attention.   **TRUE   FALSE**

6. Mental illnesses can be treated and cured.   **TRUE   FALSE**

7. People who are depressed have weak personalities; they are often lazy and
    should look at life more positively.   **TRUE   FALSE**

8. Mental illness can be 'caught'.   **TRUE   FALSE**

9. Mental illness is just like any other illness such as heart disease or arthritis. **TRUE   FALSE**

10. Mental illness is the result of poor parenting.   **TRUE   FALSE**

P   *Mental Health in Schools* by Mark Prever (2006). Paul Chapman Publishing

3. Stigma

Activity guidance notes for teachers

The word *stigma* is associated with feelings of shame or disgrace. For a person experiencing a mental health problem, the views of others affect self-esteem and can last a lifetime. Stigma can lead to discrimination, and affects relationships in potentially disastrous ways. Stigma is associated with prejudice and misunderstanding. This activity asks pupils to begin to experience what this might be like.

Time

40 minutes.

What you will need

No materials are required for the main activity, although art materials will be necessary for extension activities.

How to do it

Firstly, explore the concept of *stigma* with pupils. What does the word mean? What might be the origin of the word? The dictionary defines stigma as a mark of 'social disgrace', and of course it is linked to the Crucifixion of Jesus and subsequent claims throughout history from individuals who have claimed that wounds on their hands and feet appear to resemble those probably experienced by Jesus himself.

Ask pupils to work with a partner. They should decide who will be **A** and who will be **B**. **A** should talk for five minutes about the experience of having a mental health problem and being treated differently by other people. Ask pupils not only to 'tell their story' but also express thoughts and feelings. **B** should listen as carefully as possible, encouraging the partner to speak, without challenging or judging. You should time-keep, and after the allotted five minutes, ask the pupils to swap around. At the end of the activity, ask pupils what it felt like to be taking on the roles of speaker and listener. In the role-plays, ask the pupils to consider incorporating some of the following:

- how stigma affects their relationships at home and at school
- being treated as abnormal or 'sick'
- being afraid to tell anybody about the problem
- feelings such as anger, fear, sadness, loneliness and isolation
- effect on self-esteem

- being treated as an 'illness', and not a person

- feeling rejected, worthless and less than human.

Extension activities

There are many opportunities to explore the experience of stigma through creative activities such as poetry, stories, letter writing, poster work or art. Pupils can also be asked to explore ways in which stigma can be challenged, as through education; seeing mental illness as simply, another kind of illness; and challenging myths, misconceptions, stigmatising language and negative attitudes. They might also like to consider ways in which they can be more supportive of friends and family who may be experiencing emotional difficulty in their lives.

4. What causes a mental health problem

Activity guidance notes for teachers

Some mental health problems are related to genetic and physiological factors and are seen as having medical causes. However, many events and relationship problems might cause or maintain a person's emotional distress. This activity asks pupils to explore those factors that might have a negative and sometimes debilitating effect on a person's emotional health and well-being.

Time

50 minutes. The session can be extended to two sessions.

What you will need

- lots of newspapers and magazines

- scissors

- A3 paper

- glue.

How to do it

Have plenty of newspapers and magazines available and prepare yourself for a mess! Ask the pupils to make a collage based on the causes of mental health problems. Pictures and words can be torn or cut out and stuck on the paper without any unnecessary focus on neatness, but in a way that represents the factors that influence a person's mental health. This could take around 30 minutes. Ask for volunteers to come to the front of the room and talk through their creation.

Sometimes, there may be a tenuous link between the image and cause, but the collage is not there as an accurate record but as a means of communicating ideas. Newspapers and magazines contain pictures, images and headlines that refer to matters such as family breakdown, crime, violence, substance abuse, death, poverty, parenting styles, illness, bullying and all kinds of abuse. Make sure you leave enough time for clearing up. An alternative – and possibly more controlled – activity would be to produce your own montage of images, which could be photo-copied and discussed in small groups.

Extension activities

Pupils can be asked to keep a record of news items and storylines from soaps and dramas that touch on the factors which might affect mental health.

> ### 5. Risk and resilience
>
> **Activity guidance notes for teachers**

For a number of years, professionals have been interested in why some young people do not develop mental health problems despite their exposure to a number of *risk factors*. Risk factors merely increase the probability that a child will develop a mental health problem, and, clearly, there is a complex interplay between these potentially negative influences and what are referred to as *protective* or *resilience* factors. These activities help pupils to explore the concepts of risk and resilience and perhaps privately relate them to their own experience.

 ## Time

50 minutes.

 ## What you will need

Copies of the activity sheet 'Risk and Resilience' (page 95) for all pupils.

How to do it

The activity can be carried out in small groups or individually. Explain the concepts of risk and resilience. Ask participitants why some young people face various issues in their lives but appear to develop, thrive and progress, while the lives of others appear to fall apart, plunging them into depression and self-destructive behaviours.

Then, ask the pupils to find different ways of grouping the risk and resilience factors, or offer them the idea that they could be grouped under headings such as:

- factors within the child

- factors within the family

- factors within the community.

Now, ask the pupils to categorise both risk and resilience factors from the list provided. Inevitably, there will be some overlap, and this should facilitate interesting discussion. You could perhaps draw up a composite set of lists drawn from the pupils' deliberations that represents a kind of consensus, if indeed this is possible.

Extension activities

Give the pupils two large pieces of paper and ask them to represent risk and resilience in symbolic form. Ask pupils if factors can be ranked according to influence. This should initiate some interesting discussion.

Photocopiable

Activity 5 Activity Sheet – Risk and Resilience

Attempt to group all risk and resilience factors in a young person's life. You may wish to use the following categories or identify your own:

■ within the child

■ within the family

■ within the community.

Risk factors	Resilience factors
Poor social skills	Living in a close family
Hanging around with peers who get into trouble	Attending a good school
A parent who suffers from a mental illness	Following a religion
Being made homeless	Being a girl
Overly strict parents	A good sense of humour
Poverty	Being a loveable baby
Being involved in a natural disaster	Being clever
A rejecting mother or father	A positive attitude to life
Being the victim of racism	Taking part in sports
Lots of arguing at home	Teachers have high expectations
Suffering from a long-term illness	Lots of love and affection
Parents' divorce or separation	A high family income
The death of a parent or grandparent	Good social skills
Parent in prison	A drug-free family
Having a learning difficulty	Respect for authority
Low self-esteem	A large friendship group
Truancy from school	Good housing
Being a refugee or asylum seeker	A large extended family
Emotional abuse	Quality time with parents
Witnessing violence on the streets	Parental support for education

P *Mental Health in Schools* by Mark Prever (2006). Paul Chapman Publishing

6. Emotional health and well-being

Activity guidance notes for teachers

Emotional health and well-being are important prerequisites for young persons to function at an optimal level, achieve their full potential and enjoy life. This exercise encourages pupils to explore what might constitute emotional health and its counterpart, unhealthy functioning.

 Time

35 minutes.

 What you will need

- flip-chart paper
- felt-tip pens.

How to do it

Split the whole class into smaller sub-groups of around four pupils. Ask half of the groups to explore emotional health and the other half emotional ill-health. Distribute the pens and paper and ask the first half of the class to come up with a list of words that might describe somebody who is 'emotionally healthy'. Set aside ten minutes for this. Examples might include the following:

Enjoys life	Positive outlook
Easygoing	Has a clear sense of their future
Good at making decisions	Lives in the present
Self-confident	Has lots of energy
Happy	Looks after their appearance
Good sense of humour	Uses leisure time to the full
Sociable	Has lots of friends
Warm personality	Is a good listener

Ask the other half of the class to list words and ideas that might be associated with a person who is 'emotionally unhealthy'. For example:

Often feels anxious or afraid	Irritable or aggressive
Cries easily	Neglects their appearance
Often sad or depressed	Lethargic
Does not like eating in public	Avoids social contact
Is often tired	Displays a lot of anger
Is plagued by worrying thoughts	Fears the future
Life appears to be out of control	Bullies others
Talks about hurting themselves	Feels that problems are insoluble

Finally, ask the groups to give feedback to the whole class.

Extension activities

When looking at some of the characteristics that define emotional health, it may be useful to see them in terms of feelings, thoughts and behaviours. Ask the groups to reorder their lists under these three headings.

7. Mental illness

Activity guidance notes for teachers

This activity invites pupils to begin to understand the range of mental health problems faced by young people in particular.

Time

40 minutes.

What you will need

- a copy for each pupil of the activity sheet 'Mental Illness and Young People' (page 99)

- flip-chart paper

- felt-tip pens.

How to do it

It is important to remember that some pupils in the class may be affected directly or indirectly by the mental health problems described here. Special awareness and sensitivity is needed, and where such a connection is known, the content of the session should be discussed with the child concerned.

Ask the pupils, working in small groups, to list as many mental health problems as they can. This should take around 15 minutes. Distribute copies of the activity sheet 'Mental Illness and Young People'. Pupils are asked to link the mental health problem with the descriptions in the second column. Clearly, some generalisations are necessary, and there will inevitably be overlap in some cases.

Pupils are also asked to record what they already know about these problems.

Extension activities

There is a great deal of material available on the internet concerning the mental health problems identified here. Groups of students could be asked to research different problems and at a later stage give a presentation to the whole group. It should also be possible to use some of the information contained in this book. Mental health problems often have self-help or interest groups linked with them. These groups are a good source of information and will sometimes supply speakers or a range of teaching materials.

Photocopiable

Activity 7 Activity Sheet – Mental Illness and Young People

Young people sometimes experience a range of mental health difficulties. See if you can link the problem with the description. What else do you know about these mental illnesses?

Schizophrenia	Distressing thoughts and rituals, often necessitating repeating behaviours such as checking and washing hands
Attention-deficit and hyperactivity disorder	Repeatedly hurting oneself, often by cutting
Asperger's syndrome	Deliberately, and often secretly, restricting food intake with the intention of losing weight, often without the need to
Anorexia nervosa	Finding it hard to settle down to a task and pay attention. Sometimes disrupting others or damaging their possessions
Obsessive-compulsive disorder	Strong feelings of sadness. A loss of pleasure or interest in things once enjoyed. Feeling worthless and without hope
Post-traumatic stress disorder	Seeing the world as threatening; inability to relax and excessive worry
Anxiety	Recurrent dreams and recollections of a past event; avoiding specific activities, people and events
Conduct disorder	Characterised by major abnormalities of thinking, beliefs and perception. Sufferers often lose insight and contact with reality
Depression	Often failing to use non-verbal expression or to recognise it in others; sometimes engaging in repetitive and ritualistic activities; often lacking empathy; difficulty in making friends
Self-harm	Persistently unable to control behaviour and obey acceptable rules. Characterised by defiance of authority and challenging, sometimes destructive, behaviour

P *Mental Health in Schools* by Mark Prever (2006). Paul Chapman Publishing

8. Feelings and behaviour

Activity guidance notes for teachers

Clearly, there is a link between mental health and behaviour. This session asks pupils to begin to explore this link by looking at their own feelings and how these might have a positive or negative effect on their schoolwork and relationships with others. This is a self-awareness exercise. Explain that 'behaviour' here is not meant only in terms of conduct, but is more about what pupils do and how they act in different situations and with different people. Pupils are then asked to explore how mental health difficulties might affect a young person at school.

 ## Time

50 minutes.

 ## What you will need

- copies of the worksheet 'Feelings and Behaviour'

- pens

- flip-chart paper.

How to do it

Working alone, pupils complete Section A of the following activity sheet, 'Feelings and Behaviour'. This should take approximately 15 minutes. It asks them to record a time when they have experienced certain feelings. Pupils may want to retain confidentiality when completing this activity; therefore, responses could be recorded symbolically in a way only the pupil will understand.

Pupils then complete Section B, which asks them to describe how having certain feelings might affect their school work, friendships and relationships at home. Ask the pupils to return to the last session, which explored mental illness. How might each of these mental health problems affect a young person's behaviour and relationships with adults and pupils in school? Ask pupils to work in pairs and explore this idea in more detail.

Extension activities

Ask pupils to monitor and record their emotions over a number of days. How have these affected their behaviour? What has been the effect on others?

Photocopiable

Activity 8 Activity Sheet – Feelings and Behaviour

Section A

Try to remember a time from the recent or distant past when you have experienced the following feelings and emotions. If you prefer, you may like to record your thoughts in a way that only you can understand.

A TIME I FELT:

Really sad . . . .

Very angry . . . .

Left out . . . .

Happy . . . .

Lonely . . . .

Frightened . . . .

Tired . . . .

Confident . . . .

Stressed . . . .

Depressed . . . .

Friendly . . . .

Ashamed . . . .

Hopeless . . . .

Put down . . . .

Section B

Draw up a chart that lists these feelings and any others that come to mind. Show how experiencing these feelings might affect your behaviour:

■ at school

■ with your friends

■ at home.

How might your behaviour affect other people? How might it change their behaviour toward you?

P *Mental Health in Schools* by Mark Prever (2006). Paul Chapman Publishing

9. Feelings, mental health and learning – the connection

Activity guidance notes for teachers

When pupils feel depressed or unhappy, or when they are anxious or scared, their capacity to learn is adversely affected. They may withdraw or show aggression. Sometimes they act out. When children feel unloved or neglected, they may seek attention or give up trying. As with young people, our own ability to learn will be affected by our emotional health and well-being. Learning involves risk, and when young persons feel that their sense of worth is in jeopardy, or when they have come to expect failure, they will resist learning. These activities call upon pupils to understand these concepts and relate them to personal experience.

 # Time

45 minutes.

 # What you will need

- copies of the following 'Case Study' activity sheet for all pupils
- pens and paper.

How to do it

Explain the potential link between emotional health and learning. Ask pupils to work with a partner. Distribute the 'Case Study' activity sheet and ask them to consider the two scenarios and accompanying questions. They should record their responses in note form. After 10 minutes, ask them to join with another pair and share ideas.

Extension activities

This material could provide an opportunity for role-play. Ask the pupils to work in pairs and each take on the role of parent/teacher and pupil whose underachievement is explored. The pupils could be asked to consider, individually, times when they have avoided work at school or when their learning has been impeded by strong thoughts and feelings.

Photocopiable

Activity 9 Activity Sheet – Case Study

Case study 1

Until recently, Khalida has been a model pupil. She has had her coursework well under control and often handed it in well in advance of due dates. She has always been popular and has a number of firm friends who are also doing well. Since Year 7, her attendance and punctuality have always been exemplary, and her only significant absence was when her parents split up when she was in Year 9, and she went to live with her dad for a while. Her behaviour has always been very good, and apart from a couple of detentions for minor offences, there have been few concerns. Her grandmother has been ill for some time, and Khalida visits her regularly. Her mother has very high expectations of her academically, and she is expected to go to university after completing her A levels. However, recently, Khalida's form tutor has noticed changes. She's late once a week and seems irritable in lessons. Her English teacher has noted that she has some coursework owing, a very unusual lapse. Khalida has spent more time in the library at lunchtimes and appears to be only browsing. There was an incident last week when she was rude to a member of staff and aggressive to a dinner supervisor who insisted that she could not eat her sandwiches in the main dining hall. Importantly, Khalida seems to be bored in class and withdrawn, and she rarely contributes to discussion. Her written work is correct but minimal.

1. In what ways has Khalida changed?

2. Can you suggest what might have caused these changes?

3. What feelings might Khalida be experiencing?

4. How has her learning been affected?

Case study 2

Dean has always had difficulties. His junior school report is littered with behaviour report forms, albeit of a minor nature. He does little work in class and often remarks that the lesson is 'boring' or that it is 'too easy'. In lessons, Dean sits with three friends who are equally reluctant to engage with work most of the time. Dean regularly forgets his equipment and rarely does any homework. Dean can be quite disruptive, often engaging in activities that have no connection to his work. On some occasions, he prevents others from working by taking their pen or hiding their belongings. He often gets into an argument with Tariq, whom he regards as a 'boffin'. Dean is in Year 8, but many of his teachers expect him to be excluded by the end of Year 9.

1. What is going on for Dean?

2. Why does he find the work boring and too easy?

3. Why does he attempt to prevent others from working?

4. Why might learning be risky for Dean?

5. What is Dean feeling?

P *Mental Health in Schools* by Mark Prever (2006). Paul Chapman Publishing

10. A little help

Activity guidance notes for teachers

While most people will not experience a diagnosed mental illness, many adults and young people will feel low, depressed or anxious, and may display aspects of behaviour that, if more long-lasting, persistent and severe, may be regarded as a mental health problem. It is clear that adults and young people will need support at various points in their lives. These activities help pupils explore possibilities.

 Time

40 minutes.

What you will need

- copies for all pupils of the following activity sheet 'Who Can Help?'
- A4 paper
- pens and felt-tip pens.

How to do it

Conduct a wordstorm with the whole group about who can help young people when they have a problem. This might include:

Social workers	Teachers	Learning mentors
Head of Year	Education social workers	Parents
Friends	Grandparents	Special needs teachers
Family friends	Neighbours	Brothers and sisters
Doctors	Nurses	Psychologists
Psychiatrists	Counsellors	Behaviour support
Uncles and aunts		

Give out copies of 'Who Can Help?' and ask pupils to complete it. After five minutes, ask the pupils to share with one other person. Are any patterns discernible? What kinds of problems do we share with different kinds of people?

Extension activities

Discuss with the pupils what would prevent young people from seeking help if they felt that they might have a mental health problem? Ask pupils to interview an adult they know well to explore how that person had found help when there was an emotional need.

Photocopiable

Activty 10   Activity Sheet – Who Can Help?

Who might be able to help and support you if you were experiencing the following kinds of problems in your life? If you prefer not to answer these personally, consider your responses as advice to a friend in need.

Problem	**Who can help?**
You are being bullied at school.	. . . .
Your parents are splitting up and always arguing.	. . . .
Someone close to you has died and you can't seem to stop crying.	. . . .
You get headaches all the time.	. . . .
You are worried that you keep on losing your temper.	. . . .
You are frightened to go to school for no apparent reason.	. . . .
You are frightened to go home because of the violence.	. . . .
You know that your behaviour at home and school is getting worse and you want to turn things around.	. . . .
You have fallen out with your best friend.	. . . .
Exams are looming and you are sick with worry.	. . . .
You are making yourself sick after meals.	. . . .
You have felt that taking lots of pills would solve all your problems.	. . . .
You have felt sad and unhappy for many weeks and see no light at the end of the tunnel.	. . . .
The work at school is too hard.	. . . .

 Mental Health in Schools by Mark Prever (2006). Paul Chapman Publishing

11. A listening ear

Activity guidance notes for teachers

Many young people seek support from each other, and this is to be welcomed. Many schools have attempted to formalise this process by introducing peer support and other similar schemes. The reality is, however, that most emotional support on a personal level occurs between friends. This session encourages pupils to develop the skills of helping and also to understand when it may be necessary to involve an adult.

 ## Time

55 minutes.

What you will need

- flip-chart paper
- felt-tip pens
- space!

How to do it

Working in small groups, ask the pupils to come up with the qualities of being a good helper and listener and give feedback to the whole group. Such qualities might include:

Regard for non-verbal communication	Asking open questions
Good eye contact	Being approachable
Empathy	Offering time
Being non-judgemental	Trust
Confidentiality	Focusing on feelings
Understanding	Warmth

Ask pupils to practise some of these skills in a one-to-one situation. Pupils work in threes, each taking the role of listener, talker and observer. Each talks about a real or imagined problem for five minutes (you keep time). After each five minutes, ask the trio what it was like to talk, be listened to and to observe. This is not meant to be an exercise in counselling skills, but merely an opportunity for pupils to focus on what a good helping relationship would look and feel like.

Talk to the class about the limits to confidentiality. Pupils should consider when they might need to seek help from a caring adult and under what circumstances they might consider breaking confidentiality. This could take the form of a whole-class debate. Examples include:

- if the friend is at risk of harm in some way

- if the friend is in danger of hurting another person

- if the friend is self-harming

- if the friend is contemplating suicide or has already made an attempt

- if the friend has been or is likely to be abused, especially physically or sexually

- if the friend is displaying unusual behaviours or having disturbing thoughts

- if there is a risk of violence.

Extension activities

The group may wish to research and practise listening skills in more depth. Ask the group to identify some of the qualities of a good friend.

12. Communicating what we feel

Activity guidance notes for teachers

There is a growing interest in what may be referred to as 'emotional literacy' and in particular, how it can contribute to the emotional well-being of young people in schools. Key to emotional literacy are principles such as self-awareness and the ability to understand our own emotions and those of others. We also need to use these insights and understandings to make us more effective in our own lives. Indeed, it can be argued that emotional literacy is an important language. Put simply, the larger our vocabulary of feelings, the more able we are to express ourselves in healthy ways. The following activities encourage pupils to develop an extended feelings vocabulary and to use it in their daily lives.

 ## Time

50 minutes.

 ## What you will need

- flip-chart paper

- pens

- 'feelings sheets' (created by the teacher), listing the five key emotions (shown below).

How to do it

Split the class into five groups. Hand each group one of the 'feelings sheets'. Alternatively, you can give each pupil an individual sheet that is headed accordingly. Ask them to collectively write down as many words as they can think of associated with that key emotion; for example, anger, irritation, annoyance, fury, rage, aggression, violence and hate.

The five key emotions are

- anger
- happiness
- fear
- disgust
- sadness.

Allow ten minutes for this. Now ask them to rank them according to intensity; for example, ecstasy, joy, pleasure and amusement. Each group should present its results. Is everybody in agreement with the rankings?

Ask the class to form pairs. Each pupil talks for five minutes about something important to them in the past, present or future, using as many feeling words as possible. Pupils can take part at the level they are most comfortable with.

Extension activities

Ask each pupil to choose a letter of the alphabet and come up with as many feeling words as possible that begin with that letter. *X, Y* and *Z* could prove difficult!

Ask pupils to use feeling words consciously with family and friends for a couple of days. Do they feel better understood? How did people react?

13. A mentally healthy school

Activity guidance notes for teachers

Schools have a responsibility to promote the social and emotional development of all pupils. This activity asks pupils to identify ways in which schools already do this and how emotional health can further be supported.

 # Time

1 hour.

✎ What you will need

- large sheets of paper

- lots of coloured felt-tip pens or paints.

How to do it

Pupils should work in small groups. They should be asked to design a 'mentally healthy school'. This could be a visual representation or take the form of a large collection of illustrated ideas. Suitable areas to include are as follows:

- the building design and facilities

- leisure areas

- the canteen

- the playground

- teaching and learning

- the curriculum

- relationships between pupils

- relationships between adults and young people

- involvement with parents and carers

- support staff for pupils

- involvement of outside agencies

- resources

- policies, especially those relating to bullying, behaviour, drugs and sex education.

Each group could be asked to introduce their 'ideal' school to the whole group.

An alternative, which requires some confidence, is to ask pupils to begin their activity by identifying the characteristics of a mentally 'unhealthy' school. On completion, these negatives can be reversed to form the mentally healthy school.

Extension activities

Pupils can produce publicity with a computer to advertise the mentally healthy school. A TV or radio advert could be written and recorded or performed.

Ideas for improvements in the school could be submitted to the school council.

14. Questions in a box

Activity guidance notes for teachers

At the end of this course, pupils may be left with a whole range of feelings and issues that have not been addressed or that have affected them more than expected. These final activities offer the class an opportunity to ask questions and explore feelings. As with the rest of the course, it is important to have suitable support systems in place to help pupils in need.

 Time

25 minutes.

 What you will need

- a medium-sized cardboard box
- pieces of card or paper.

How to do it

Ask pupils to write down any comments, feelings or questions they might have about this work on mental health. These can be anonymous, or the pupils may, if they wish, write their name. The slips should all be placed in the box. The teacher should mix them up and read them to the class. No pupils' names should be read out. Pupils can ask for their card not to be read out by marking it with a cross. In many ways, this is an opportunity for pupils to evaluate and reflect upon the course. However, if pupils want further help, this is one way in which they can ask for support.

CHAPTER 8

The listening school

> This chapter will show:
>
> Really listening to young people is the most important way in which we can help pupils with mental health problems and also promote emotional health and well-being in schools. It is, of course, important to distinguish between the use of listening skills and counselling, which is a more specialised activity. All young people should be able to access counselling in schools as an entitlement, but the introduction of such a service needs to be thought through and many issues and practicalities explored.

Listening skills and counselling

Experience has taught me that, regardless of the child and despite the young person's present predicament, real listening is the most profound way in which to help a young person. As professionals we are often impotent when it comes to changing many of the difficulties that young people experience. We cannot lift a family from poverty, remove a sibling with a severe disability from the home, bring back a lost parent or stop parents from tearing each other apart, but we can listen. Reference to our own experience will tell us that sometimes all we need to know is that somebody really understands what we are experiencing. I do believe that teachers and other adults in school are well placed to offer this kind of attention, and some do willingly. I am also aware that sometimes we claim to be listening when what we are really doing is offering guidance and advice. These are valid interventions but they do not represent real listening. Indeed, the very term 'counselling' is misused in schools and, at worst, can be entirely distorted – as when we hear the suggestion that a pupil with behaviour problems needs 'counselling'.

I believe that genuine non-judgemental listening in schools is rare – and beautiful where it is found. The use of counselling skills should not be confused with counselling, which is a different and more specialised activity with different boundaries and processes. Counselling involves the setting up of a specific contract between a trained counsellor and persons who understand that they are in the role of client. Good listening can occur at any appropriate time and often where there is an available space. Counselling, by contrast, takes place in the same place, normally on a weekly basis for a fixed period of time. Depending upon the model used, the counsellor will work in a particular way, using well-established theory and ideas attached to that particular theoretical model. There will also be a clear understanding of the therapeutic nature of the work. However, teachers and other school-based staff, whilst not normally trained counsellors, can develop, refine and use counselling skills to good effect. Real listening cuts through most things, and I believe it is possible to find the real child in every young person, despite the behaviours that make them hard to reach or sometimes encourage us to reject or despise them.

What constitutes good listening?

Carl Rogers (1902–1987), a humanistic counsellor and psychotherapist, set out clearly what he regarded as the 'core conditions' that are essential in any therapeutic relationship. Rogers's (1951) ideas have had a profound and long-lasting influence on the world of counselling, but his ideas are equally applicable for use by non-specialists. They set out the basis for good listening.

The three core conditions are the following:

- *congruence*
  This is the honest relationship between people's inner feelings and their outer display. Congruence may therefore be seen as not 'playing a role' but being real, genuine and transparent.

- *unconditional positive regard*
  This means offering a person your full, caring attention without judgement or evaluation.

- *empathy*
  This refers to seeing the world through another person's eyes and accepting that person's perceptions and feelings 'as if' they are your own without losing your boundaries and separate sense of self.

These core conditions, Rogers believed, help people find their own way, identify their own solutions and grow personally. They are easy to say, and even to write about, but these ideas represent the most sophisticated of human interpersonal skills. Only when you have experienced them is it possible really to understand what it feels like to be listened to. As teachers, we rarely offer this kind of listening, but there is no reason why we cannot. The following list also sets out what good listening might look like.

Photocopiable

What constitutes good listening?

- Understand the feelings, not only the content, of what is being said. Sometimes this may involve looking beyond the stated word.

- Acknowledge and identify what pupils might be feeling and offer this to them.

- Recognise and communicate that talking about a problem may be difficult for the young person; it may be especially and uniquely painful.

- Be accepting. Work to receive genuinely what the young person is telling you, even if you are thinking and feeling differently, have different values or see the situation from a position of experience. Do not stop listening because you do not agree.

- Be genuinely interested and demonstrate this. We can communicate interest by maintaining eye contact, not fidgeting and not asking too many questions; our posture and minimal responses should show we are trying to understand and want the young person to continue telling the story.

- Offer as much confidentiality as you can within child-protection guidelines. Thoughts and feelings about home and school do not always need to be shared. Explore with the pupil the limitations of what can remain private from the outset and return to these periodically. This gives the young person control over disclosure.

- Be available. Let pupils know that it is OK to talk to you.

- Listen patiently.

- Make time and space for real listening to happen. Listen with your full attention, not whilst doing something else.

- Be aware of your own feelings and recognise when the pupil's words or story resonate with your own material or experience.

- Be comfortable with anger as long as it is expressed in words and feelings, and not in physically destructive ways. Anger represents feelings which are unexpressed or not heard.

- Where appropriate, say what you are feeling. Model how to share emotions.

- Believe what young persons say. This is how they see it at this moment in time.

- Do not interrupt; your role is to facilitate talk.

- Do not assume you know what the young person is saying.

- Always remain calm when the pupil is sharing with you.

- Ask few questions; those that you do ask should be open-ended in order to elicit more than a one-word or 'yes' or 'no' answer.

P *Mental Health in Schools* by Mark Prever (2006). Paul Chapman Publishing

- Rather than offer solutions, help the young person to identify options. Person-centred theory is based upon the idea that ultimately we know what is best for us and given the right conditions we will find our own way. Good listening will help pupils to identify options and decide a course of action. Experience has taught me that solutions suggested or imposed are resisted, short-term or only agreed to by the young person in order to maintain relationships or 'please' the helper. Solutions come from a frame of reference based upon a range of experiences very different from those of the young person being listened to.

- Maintain good eye contact unless this is experienced as threatening.

- Be comfortable with silence. It may be that the young person needs to think or feel.

- Try to paraphrase what the pupil is telling you. This communicates that you are really listening.

- Be an attentive listener. Use a variety of brief responses, such as nodding your head, or saying 'uh-huh', 'I see', 'go on', 'what happened next?', and 'how did it make you feel?', to communicate that you are listening and to encourage the pupil to continue.

- Listen with your eyes. Facial expressions, body posture and arm movements tell what is really going on for the young person.

- Be prepared to admit your limitations and refer on when you feel young persons are at risk or that what they are telling you makes you feel 'out of your depth'. If you are concerned, be prepared to say so. It is important to remember that when you support a pupil in this way you are part of a wider pastoral system within the school, and other people should be aware of what you are doing. For your own professional safety, it is important to listen to a pupil in a place which can be overlooked by and is accessible to colleagues, but not by pupils' peers.

P *Mental Health in Schools* by Mark Prever (2006). Paul Chapman Publishing

Photocopiable

Barriers to effective listening

- moralising or preaching, as if we are in a place of worship

- lecturing, as if to a group of students

- giving advice as a consultant might do

- offering suggestions from our perspective

- mind reading as in a theatre performance

- filtering (hearing only what we want to hear)

- being judgemental or critical because we know what is best

- daydreaming or thinking about our evening meal or when to do the shopping

- becoming preoccupied with what we are going to say next, thereby missing what the young person is actually saying

- interrupting or filling a silence when there is a natural pause or the need for reflection, mainly because we are feeling uncomfortable

- rescuing, reassuring, sympathising or praising to make pupils feel better without having an opportunity to express what they are experiencing. (Actually what we may be doing is making ourselves feel better, rather than staying with the pain and hurt.)

- questioning or interrogating as if interviewing a suspected criminal

- trying to please pupils because we have become dependent upon their approval

- intellectualising (listening with the head and not the heart) (Intellectualisation releases us from the need to experience the feelings within ourselves or those of the young person. Intellectualisation offers safety but can prevent real listening and prevent the young persons from really experiencing what they are saying.)

- remembering our own life experiences as we listen (This can lead to over-identification and distort the helping process.)

- using humour or changing the subject when uncomfortable emotions or feelings are aroused (These may be our own defence mechanisms in operation protecting our vulnerable or raw self.)

- pseudo-listening (being preoccupied with what is happening inside our own head or in the room)

- making notes as the young person talks (Notes can be written up afterward. Writing is distracting to the listener and does not indicate attention to the young person telling their story.)

- listening only for facts and becoming preoccupied with structure and chronology (Whilst these may be important, the young person would rarely have experienced an opportunity to talk about their feelings.).

© British Association for Counselling and Psychotherapy 2006 (BACP)

P *Mental Health in Schools* by Mark Prever (2006). Paul Chapman Publishing

Peer-support schemes

Schools have informally recognised the natural tendency for young people to offer each other support and friendship, particularly in times of crisis or periods of transition. Indeed, it could be argued that young people often seek out their peers first in times of difficulty, rather than turning to parents and teachers. Peer-support schemes recognise these processes and seek to harness this natural humanity found in young people. Space prohibits giving detailed procedures for setting up a scheme, but a number of publications by ChildLine (2002; 2004) form good starting points for schools seriously considering introducing a scheme of some kind.

Peer-support schemes take a number of forms, each with a different focus but equally valuable. These include:

- friendship, befriending or 'buddying'

- mentoring

- conflict resolution or mediation

- peer listening.

I have used the term *peer listening* in preference to the sometimes used *peer counsellor*, which I believe is risky, in that it implies a specific professional role requiring significant training and experience. To refer to peer supporters as 'counsellors' suggests an activity that has expectations beyond maturity.

All of these contribute to the idea of a listening school. They often exist alongside and complement other listening ideas such as the school council and circle time.

Natalie Tormey (2005) sets out clearly some of the benefits of peer-support schemes. Pupils benefit from non-judgemental listening and 'help, comfort and guidance' which arise from wider social networks. Teachers see their school improve and appreciate the introduction of an additional level of support that is often neglected through lack of time. Young people participating as peer supporters gain self-confidence, improve their communication skills, and develop socially and personally themselves. Finally, Tormey sets out whole-school benefits of such schemes, which include reduced levels of bullying, the approval of parents, better behaviour and improvements in educational attainment.

The following checklist represents some of the key questions and issues that will need to be addressed if such a scheme is to be introduced. Cowie and Wallace (2000) set out the potential of such undertakings but also highlight the possible dangers if such projects are not introduced with care and considerable thought.

Photocopiable

Setting up a peer-support programme: questions to consider

- Has the school sufficient financial, staffing and spatial resources for such an undertaking? Would a special budget be set aside? Clearly, there are implications for time and space, but the project needs a relatively low budget, perhaps a few hundred pounds in the first instance, if only to signal to participants that the scheme is valued and give peer supporters a say in the development of the scheme.

- Is there firm support and encouragement from the senior leadership team for the scheme?

- How would a peer-support scheme fit into the general school ethos? Are there compatible values between the main school and the idea of empowering young people in this way? Certainly, a number of the elements of the PSE/citizenship curriculum, the National Healthy Schools Award and the **Every Child Matters** initiative can be addressed by a comprehensive peer-support programme.

- How would such a scheme fit into the school's wider pastoral care system? Pastoral managers need to be supportive and kept informed. Preferably, they should be involved in the development and implementation of the project. Involve them from the start.

- Which kind of peer-support scheme best fits the needs of your school? It would be useful to have some discussion as to where most support is needed. Is bullying an issue? Do new pupils feel safe and secure? What other provision is made for pupils to share their problems? Answers to questions such as these will help your school decide on the most appropriate model.

- How will peer supporters be trained, and by whom? Do these persons need specialist experience and qualifications? Could such expertise be brought in? In my experience, it is best to work with other agencies, such as a youth-counselling organisation with experience of training. Because of the nature of the work, a few days off-site training would be an excellent investment.

- As peer helpers will need regular supervision, which has time implications, who is qualified and able to offer this kind of support? Supervision is a necessary and important component in any successful scheme and one sometimes neglected. Perhaps an experienced counselling supervisor could be brought in to work with groups of peer supporters. Supervision should not be confused with daily monitoring and the management of individuals within the project.

- Where will this work take place? Are there rooms that offer a degree of privacy and are regularly available? Peer supporters need a safe place in which to work. Pupils are unlikely to seek out support in full view of their peers, who may see seeking help as a sign of weakness.

- How will peer listeners be selected or recruited? What qualities are desirable? Should these young people apply for these responsibilities or be approached directly? Peer supporters need to offer a degree of maturity and confidence. They need to be good listeners and display empathy. They need to be approachable, reliable and organised. As with counselling, peer supporters may not be able to offer full attention to the needs of others if they are in crisis themselves. Sometimes pupils may be approached directly or identified by staff, but I believe that these important roles carry more credibility when the posts are advertised and full, often practical selection procedures are used. Again, a local counselling agency, used to recruiting volunteers, may be more than willing to help.

▶

P *Mental Health in Schools* by Mark Prever (2006). Paul Chapman Publishing

■ How might the scheme be viewed by other staff and parents? Might some professionals in school find it threatening? Peer supporters need to feel valued, and staff need to be on board from the start. The programme should be discussed with all staff after the decision has been made to explore the possibilities of such a project. Some staff may feel that the project may take students away from their main task of learning and achieving results; others may feel that it is open to manipulation by pupils. Some staff may even fear that they might be the subject of discussion. However, in my experience, adults in school are highly supportive of such ventures, and the more organised, defined and transparent the scheme is, the better.

■ How should the scheme be advertised and made known to other pupils? Talks in assembly? Photographs displayed around the school? Posters advertising the scheme? Sometimes, peer supporters can introduce themselves during tutor time or with small groups of pupils.

■ Will the scheme focus on certain year groups, such as Year 7, or be targeted at specific vulnerable groups, such as isolated or bullied pupils? Either way, it is important to be clear about this and probably best to start small and build.

■ What sort of age gap is necessary between peer supporters and their 'clients'? As stated above, a degree of maturity is necessary for this role and age may be a factor. Younger pupils, say, Year 8, could work with new intake pupils in September, but normally a suitable age difference is desirable.

■ How can we ensure that the expectations upon peer supporters will not adversely affect older pupils working toward examinations? The role of pupil and peer listener can easily coexist but requires commitment, personal effectiveness and organisation.

■ Would it be a good idea to attach to younger pupils peer supporters who have experienced similar difficulties, such as behaviour problems? This may be appropriate but there should be realistic expectations about outcomes, and pupils need to be carefully chosen.

■ Should access to peer supporters be open, by referral, or informal? The best kind of support is that which is sought voluntarily, but it is sometimes possible to make pupils aware of the support on offer and direct them as such.

■ Have issues of confidentiality and its limits been considered carefully? Training of peer listeners should include information and procedures about child protection as well as an opportunity to explore practice through role-plays. In actual fact, when there is any doubt, peer supporters should always consult with their supervisor or manager of the project. We cannot expect young people to make decisions about child abuse; this is our responsibility.

■ Has attention been paid to boundaries and to ensuring that participants in the scheme are aware of the importance of firm boundaries? In particular, this is to protect the peer supporters, who may become overwhelmed with the attention of pupils in need. Problems sometimes occur if young persons become overattached to their helper or seek a friendship which is beyond the expectations of the role. Such matters should be addressed in supervision or with the scheme manager. These difficulties may have more to do with the peer supporter not maintaining boundaries than with the supported pupil. The maintenance of boundaries remains the responsibility of the peer supporter, but always with our support.

■ Child protection is crucial — are those setting up such a scheme confident that peer supporters know how to receive possible disclosures and know exactly what to do? It is advisable to give peer supporters specific written guidance to refer to when in doubt. Peer supporters should be told to err on the side of caution and discuss concerns with an appropriate adult in the school.

■ When will the scheme operate? Lunchtime? Before and after school? Might pupils be taken out of normal lessons, especially where mediation may prevent problems from escalating? Most schools operate schemes during out-of-lesson times so as to avoid any disruption to schooling. It is also a time when pupils feel least conspicuous and are possibly most vulnerable.

■ How will the school keep peer supporters motivated after the initial enthusiasm has waned? The role of peer listener can be exhausting and will make personal demands upon the young person. Like any new initiative, morale needs to be maintained by praise, recognition, celebration and even additional training and development opportunities.

■ Do interested staff have the time and energy to keep this endeavour going? No doubt, the points made above apply equally to the adult in the school, who will probably have invested a great deal of energy and commitment to the success of the peer project.

■ What sort of records of use will be kept? How will the scheme be monitored and evaluated? What would constitute success criteria? At this level, only minimal records need to be kept. These may include details about age, ethnicity, gender and presenting problems, identified by a code, which later can be collated to provide evidence of the range, usage and value of the scheme.

■ What are the benefits for peer supporters and how might their commitment be formally recognised? The peer supporters group should meet together regularly, and refreshments should be provided. They may wish to have badges and their photographs displayed. Parents should be involved in any recognition ceremonies, and records of pupils' commitment should be passed on to future employers and colleges.

 Mental Health in Schools by Mark Prever (2006). Paul Chapman Publishing

The above section can only raise questions and suggest ideas. Each school is different, and therefore each peer-support scheme should be a good fit for each individual school, expressing its ethos, climate, relationships and priorities.

Employing a counsellor in your school

Whilst pastoral care has a long tradition in UK schools, originating in our nineteenth-century public school system, the idea of school counselling is a relatively new one. The late 1960s and early 1970s saw a growing interest in counselling, due to ideas that had been imported from the United States, and specialist training courses were set up in a number of universities, such as Keele and Reading, to produce the counsellors to meet this growing demand. Fear and suspicion of a new way of working with young people, therapeutic theory which was beyond the experience of most people, and eventual financial cutbacks in the 1970s ensured that the new profession would not reach maturity. However, in recent years, there has been a sharp rise in the number of schools offering counselling either directly or through contracts with other agencies such as the NSPCC.

This is not surprising, as the idea of counselling for young people has increasingly become part of the language of government, and schools have increasingly recognised that more traditional forms of pastoral care are sometimes ill-prepared to offer the kind of specialist support that young people need. In addition, there is a growing body of research that points clearly to evidence that counselling in schools does make a difference. I believe that there is a great unmet need for counselling in educational settings, and I want to advance the case that all schools should ensure that pupils have access to this kind of in-depth support.

The British Association for Counselling and Psychotherapy (BACP) has for years put the case for school counselling, and Counselling Children and Young People (CCYP) – the specialist division of BACP – continues to push for a counsellor in every school.

A number of pioneer LEAs have, in the past, offered counselling through a centrally funded, school counselling service. Dudley LEA has been particularly innovative over the years. Today, counselling is finding its way into schools in a variety of creative ways, including consortiums, the youth service, the voluntary sector, and services that are coordinated by the LEA but which use devolved monies to buy such services into schools. Many schools have opted to simply buy in an independent counsellor from their own funds. This remains a popular way to offer the benefits of an on-site service.

BACP (2005) defines counselling as follows: *Counselling and psychotherapy is a contractual arrangement by which a practitioner meets a client, in privacy and confidence, to explore distress the client may be experiencing. This may be a difficulty; their dissatisfaction with life; or loss of a sense of direction and purpose.*

BACP (2001) also suggests that, with regard to young people: *Counselling is a process which assists that individual client to focus on their particular concerns and developmental issues, whilst simultaneously addressing and exploring specific problems, making choices, coping with crises, working through feelings of inner conflict and improving relationships with others.*

Interviews need to test more than theoretical understanding. Essentially, the school should be looking for training, experience and the personal qualities. It would be useful to get a local counselling organisation, familiar with the selection of counsellors, to assist with the process, which should include interview activities designed to demonstrate the applicant's skills and personal qualities.

There exists some debate as to the importance of specific experience of working with young people. I consider this to be a real asset in any selection process. Certainly, any potential counsellor employed by the school should have some knowledge of this client group and the developmental issues common to this age group. School-based experience is useful to enable the school counsellor successfully to negotiate many of the potential difficulties of working in this complex setting.

Job specification

A school counsellor should have a contract that sets out the role of the counsellor in relation to pupils, parents and the school. It should cover matters such as:

- liaison with staff and outside agencies

- the setting up of the service, including referral and appointment systems

- counselling hours

- supervision

- record keeping and reporting on the service

- confidentiality and child protection

- training.

Dual roles

It is not recommended that the school counsellor be in another role at the same time, such as teacher or mentor, as this will inevitably lead to complex boundary issues and conflicting role expectations. It is also felt that, whilst professionals such as Connexions workers and nurses may use counselling skills very effectively as part of their work, they should not be operating as counsellors with some of the pupils referred to them by the school.

Supervision

All counsellors are required to have regular clinical supervision. This normally amounts to a minimum of $1^1/_2$ hours per month. Supervision may be on a one-to-one basis or in small groups. It may be paid for by the school, the contributing agency or the self-employed counsellor. Supervision is the formal overseeing of the counsellor's work with the young person, and seeks to ensure that the counsellor is working ethically and that professional standards are maintained, thereby serving to protect the client. Supervision offers counsellors an opportunity to explore their work with an experienced professional, often with additional training.

Supervision also has a supportive, developmental and educative role and acts as the bridge between theoretical knowledge and practice. Working without supervision would be deemed to be unethical, and supervision is therefore an essential requirement.

Insurance

Whilst school personnel may be covered by professional organisations and the school authorities, it is strongly recommended that counsellors have additional professional indemnity insurance from insurers specialising in this kind of protection. This is especially important due to the nature of work with young people and an increasingly litigious culture that places counsellors at risk of claims of negligence and malpractice. The counsellor, if an employee of the LEA, may be covered for insurance purposes in the normal way, but it may be best to check first. With regard to addition liability insurance, BACP would be pleased to offer information on companies offering such cover.

Information about the service

Information about the counselling service specific to the school should be included in all appropriate policies and handbooks. Counsellors should design, possibly with pupil involvement, user-friendly leaflets explaining the service and make them readily available, and pupils and parents should be aware of the availability of the school counsellor through assemblies, parent consultation evenings and governors' reports. Pupils can be made aware of the service by posters around the school, talks in assembly time or counsellors introducing themselves to the young people in groups over a period of time.

Rooms and facilities

The school will need to provide a safe, comfortable and soundproof room where sessions are unlikely to be interrupted. The room should not be a teaching area or office that has other associations for the pupil. The room should be available at the same times each week and have a secured cabinet for the storage of confidential papers. A confidential telephone line should ideally be available for counsellors to make calls to referrers and supervisors. A notice outside the room should indicate when a session – normally not identified as a counselling session – is in process.

Referral procedures

Counselling should be a voluntary activity, and pupils should not be required to attend sessions against their will. At the very least, such coercion may prove to be counterproductive. Similarly, participation in counselling should not be used as a threat or used against pupils, should they find themselves facing permanent exclusion from school. Problem behaviour would not normally constitute an appropriate referral, although, as this book has argued, many young people displaying difficult behaviour may well be facing significant problems in their lives that may be affecting their mental health and well-being. If a pupil is not happy to see a counsellor, an alternative intervention should be tried.

Referrals can be made by teachers, pastoral staff or parents, although if a school feels confident, self-referral should be encouraged. It may be useful for the school to identify a member of staff to liaise directly with the counsellor over referrals.

Appointment systems

The school counsellor should ensure that the appointment system is as discreet as possible, but also needs to recognise the complex nature of schools; thus, 'appointment slips' and ways of recording attendance will need to be introduced to ensure support from teaching staff. The most confidential appointment system is that which takes place in the counselling room when meeting times are agreed. As most schools operate computerised roll-call and registration systems, an appropriate code could be recorded to explain absence from particular lessons.

Parental consent

At present, pupils have a right to access counselling without their parents' prior knowledge or consent. This principle has been accepted for a number of years because of what has been referred to as the Gillick principle: *As a general principle it is legal and acceptable for a young person to ask for confidential counselling without parental consent, provided they are of sufficient understanding and intelligence* (*Gillick* v. *West Norfolk AHA*, House of Lords, 1985). However, it is felt that as a matter of good practice, parental consent should be established wherever possible. In most cases, parents are only too willing to agree to support for their child, especially where they, too, have been concerned about their son or daughter. It is rare for a pupil to insist on parents not knowing, and there would need to be clear reasons why the work might proceed without the parents knowing. In such circumstances, the head teacher would normally take responsibility for this decision. Some schools have added the precaution of including a statement in the annual prospectus highlighting the existence of a counsellor in the school and pupils' right to confidential access.

Timing of sessions

Adult sessions normally last for the 'therapeutic hour' of 50 minutes. In schools, it will be less, normally 35–40 minutes, depending upon the age of the pupil. Whilst the regularity of sessions each week is crucial to the therapeutic relationship and work, some schools vary the times when a young person is withdrawn from lessons so that the pupil does not miss the same lesson each week, and to avoid the disapproval of staff teaching that young person. Some schools may offer drop-in sessions at out-of-lesson times, but holding full counselling sessions during the lunch break may be resented by young persons because it prevents them from socialising with friends and deprives them of time to eat, and sessions at this time are more likely to be disturbed by other pupils. In my experience, teaching staff are highly supportive of the help offered by counsellors and are keen to collaborate in the best interests of the young person in difficulty. Some counsellors work open-endedly, but the most recent trend is to work to a fixed number of sessions.

Record keeping

Counsellors keep case notes and may also keep personal 'process' notes that record their thoughts and feelings in relation to their work. Both counsellors and schools need to be aware that legislation has given pupils over the age of 16 and parents access to educational records, and this needs to be borne in mind when establishing the school counselling service. I believe it is best to keep notes to an absolute minimum, and the counsellor should be cognisant of the fact that notes may be read by interested parties. Notes should record only a summary of the session or key words and ideas. These notes are retained and stored safely by the counsellor, who is responsible for them. They should not be included as part of the child's normal school file. Computer files may record session times and dates and when counselling ends. It should be recorded in policy that other staff in the school do not have access to these notes except in extreme circumstances and with the authority of the head teacher and the agreement of the counsellor. BACP would be happy to offer more detailed guidance in this area.

Boundaries

The maintenance of tight boundaries is an important component of all good counselling and is essential in the establishment and maintenance of a strong therapeutic alliance. Boundaries are in effect the ground rules of counselling and define clearly, among other things, the structure and timing of sessions, confidentiality and its limitations, forms of contact and – especially important in the context of schools – the nature of the relationship between the counsellor and client. This must have limits, and contact outside sessions is likely to prove unhelpful and adversely affect the quality of work in sessions. Counsellors, therefore, need to be clear with pupils from the outset that they are not normally accessible until the next scheduled session.

Confidentiality

The establishment of high levels of confidentiality is fundamental to building sufficient trust for young persons to explore their innermost thoughts and feelings with an adult. The school counsellor needs to establish clear working principles in relation to such matters as child protection, sexual activity, suspected pregnancy, crime and drug misuse. Again, BACP would be pleased to field enquiries relating to this complex legal area.

The courts

Courts are often sensitive to the role of the counsellor, but it should be understood that the courts can access counselling notes and records. Whilst counsellors are not *necessarily* required to appear in court with these papers, they can be required to do so by court order. Notes may also be requested in family court proceedings, as in custody disputes and adoption hearings.

Child protection

Counsellors working in schools are expected to work within child-protection guidelines established by the local authority. If a disclosure has been made or if they believe that a pupil is 'at risk', they will normally explain to the young person why a referral needs to be made and gain their agreement. Where a referral is made against the pupil's wishes, it is good practice to inform the client that information is going to be shared with other agencies, and details of those agencies should ideally be given to the pupil.

Feedback to the senior leadership team

Whilst specific counselling outcomes with particular pupils may remain confidential, the school counsellor should be expected to provide information about the service, including details of appointments, use of the service by different year groups, and use by gender and ethnicity. It is also useful for the counsellor to record statistically the kinds of client issues presented, especially where these may turn attention to the need for school-based action, as in the incidence of bullying or exam stress.

Reflection box

◆ To what extent is your school a 'listening school'?

◆ What kind of listener are you? How can you improve?

◆ What peer projects already exist in your school?

◆ Does your school offer pupils counselling?

◆ What personal and professional issues might emerge for you if a school counsellor were appointed to support pupils with mental health problems in your school? How would such an appointment be received by your colleagues?

USEFUL ORGANISATIONS AND RESOURCES

The following organisations, websites and contacts offer a wide variety of useful information, resources and services that can be of great use to the school concerned for the mental health and emotional well-being of its pupils. Please feel free to email me directly: markdavidprever@yahoo.co.uk.

General

Advisory Centre for Education (ACE)

A charity offering information about state education, dealing with bullying, SEN and exclusions. Offers advice, publications, training and membership.

1c Aberdeen Studios, 22 Highbury Grove, London N5 2DQ
enquiries@ace.dialnet.com
 www.ace-ed.org

Antidote

Emotional literacy organisation. Antidote works collaboratively with schools, offers training and publishes in the area of emotional literacy.

45 Beech Street, London EC2Y 8AZ
 Tel: 020 7588 5151; Fax: 020 7588 4900
Antidote@geo2.poptel.org.uk
 www.antidote.org.uk

@ease

A website-based mental health resource for young people. @ease provides advice, support and information, and works to break down stigma attached to mental illness.

 National advice line: 020 8974 6814
www.rethink.org/at-ease

BACP (British Association for Counselling and Psychotherapy)

Leading professional body for counselling and psychotherapy and an automatic reference point for anyone seeking information on these fields.

BACP House, 35–37 Albert Street, Rugby, Warwickshire CV21 2SG
 Tel: 0870 443 5252; Fax: 0870 443 5160
 www.bacp.co.uk

British Association of Psychotherapists

Specialist psychotherapy organisation offering training and setting professional standards for clinical practice.

37 Mapesbury Road, London NW2 4HJ
Tel: 020 8452 9823
www.bap-psychotherapy.org

British Psychological Society

A body which represents psychologists and psychology in the UK. BPS encourages the development of psychology as a science and profession, seeks to raise standards of training and practice, and hopes to raise public awareness.

St Andrews House, 48 Princess Road East, Leicester LE1 7DR
Tel: 0116 254 9568
www.bps.org.uk

CareLine

Provides confidential counselling and support to young people and adults, including those in crisis.

Cardinal Heenan Centre, 326 High Road, Ilford IG1 1QP
 Tel: 020 8514 1177
www.webhealth

CCYP (Counselling Children and Young People)

BACP division with a particular focus on children and young people. Holds regular conferences, offers advice and publishes a journal.

Contact Gemma Green, Divisional Administrator:
gemma.green@bacp.co.uk

ChildLine

Free 24-hour helpline for children in distress or danger. Also publishes an outreach service to schools. Young people can phone ChildLine on 0800 111 or write to: ChildLine, Freepost 111, London N1 OBR.

 www.childline.org.uk

Contact a Family

A charity providing advice, information and support to the parents of all disabled children.

209–211 City Road, London EC1V 1JN

 Tel: 020 7608 8700; helpline: 0808 808 3555

www.cafamily.org.uk

Department for Education and Skills

Sanctuary Buildings, Great Smith Street, London SW1 3BT

Tel: 0870 000 2288

info@dfes.gsi.gov.uk

Department of Health

Richmond House, 79 Whitehall, London SW1A 2NS

Tel: 020 7210 4850

dhmail@doh.gsi.gov.uk

 www.doh.gov.uk

Institute of Psychiatry

A postgraduate research and teaching institution concerned with the treatment of mental disorders.

King's College London, De Crespigny Park, London SE5 8AF

 Tel: 020 7836 5454

www.mentalhealthcare.org.uk/

Mental Health Foundation

Important mental health organisation involved in media work, publication and information.

9th Floor, Sea Containers House, 20 Upper Ground, London, SE1 9QB

Tel: 020 7803 1100; Fax: 020 7803 1111

mhf@mhf.org.uk

 www.mentalhealth.org.uk/peer

Mental Health Media

Seeks to reduce discrimination on mental health grounds by promoting the diversity, visibility and credibility of people who experience mental distress. Offers a range of media resources.

356 Holloway Road, London N7 6PA
Tel: 020 7700 8171
info@mhmedia.com

Mentality

134–138 Borough High Street, London SE1 1LB
Tel: 020 7716 6777
www.mentality.org.uk

Mind

A leading mental health charity addressing the needs of people with mental health problems. Offers information and publications, and seeks to influence policy through campaigning and education.

15 Broadway, London E15 4BQ
Tel: 020 8519 2122; information line: 0845 766 0163
www.mind.org.uk

Mind Out

An awareness and action campaign seeking to bring about changes in attitudes and behaviour surrounding mental health.

Freepost LON15335, London SE1 1BR
www.mindout.clarity.uk.net/

National Association for Pastoral Care in Education

An interest organisation concerned with school-based pastoral care and personal and social education. It produces a journal.

c/o Institute of Education, University of Warwick, Coventry CV4 7AL
Tel: 024 7652 3810; Fax: 024 7657 3031
napce@napce.org.uk

National Children's Bureau

Promotes the voices, interests and well-being of children and young people. The organisation works with children and young people, promotes cross-agency partnerships and influences policy development and research.

8 Wakley Street, London EC1V 7QE
 Tel: 020 7843 6000; Fax: 020 7278 9512
 www.ncb.org

NHS Direct

 0845 46 47.
www.nhsdirect.nhs.uk/

NSPCC

The leading charity specialising in child protection and the prevention of cruelty to children. Work includes face-to-face child protection work, a 24-hour helpline, public education campaigns, parliamentary campaigning, training and advice, research and information.

Weston House, 42 Curtain Road, London EC21 3NH
 Tel: 0808 800 5000 (24-hour helpline)
 www.nspcc.org.uk

ParentLinePlus

Offers a range of services providing help and support for parents of all kinds.

3rd Floor, Chapel House, 18 Hatton Place, London EC1N 8RU
Tel: 0808 800 2222
www.parentline.co.uk

Relate

The UK's largest provider of relationship counselling and sex therapy.

Herbert Gray College, Little Church Street, Rugby, Warwickshire CV21 3AP
 Tel: 01788 573 241; Fax: 01788 535 007
www.relate.org.uk

Rethink

Information, support and advice for people suffering from mental illness, their carers and professionals.

28 Castle Street, Kingston-Upon-Thames, Surrey KT1 1SS
☎ General enquiries Tel: 0845 456 0455
🖰 www.rethink.com
info@rethink.org

Royal College of Psychiatrists

The main professional and educational body for psychiatrists in the UK.

17 Belgrave Square, London SW1X 8PG
☎ Tel: 020 7235 2351; Fax: 20 7245 1231
🖰 www.rcpsych.ac.uk

Rural Minds

A Mind initiative with a particular interest in mental health in rural settings.

c/o South Staffs CVS, 1 Stafford Street, Brewood, Staffs ST19 9DX
☎ Tel: 01902 850060
🖰 www.mind.org.uk/About+Mind/Networks/ruralMinds/
ruralminds@ruralnet.org.uk

Sainsbury Centre for Mental Health

Research and training aiming to influence policy and practice in health and social care.

134–138 Borough High Street, London SE1 1LB
☎ Tel: 020 7827 8300
contact@scmh.org.uk

Samaritans

Crisis telephone counselling for people of all ages in distress or who may be considering suicide.

10 The Grove, Slough, Berks SL1 1QP
☎ Tel: 08457 909090 (24-hour helpline)
🖰 www.samaritans.org.uk
jo@samaritans.org

SaneLine

Offers emotional and crisis support for people suffering from mental illness. Provides information for professionals and organisations working in the mental health field.

1st Floor, Cityside House, 40 Adler Street, London E1 1EE

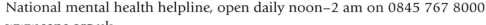 National mental health helpline, open daily noon–2 am on 0845 767 8000

www.sane.org.uk

Self-Esteem Network

32 Carisbrooke Road, Walthamstow, London E17 7EF

Stonewall

A campaigning organisation working to address prejudice and issues of equality for gay, lesbian and bisexual people.

46 Grosvenor Gardens, London SW1W 0EB

 Tel: 020 7881 9440

www.stonewall.org.uk

Teacher Support Network/TeacherLine

A free information, support and counselling service for teachers.

Hamilton House, Mabledon Place, London WC1H 9BE

 Tel: 08000 562 561 (24-hour helpline); 020 7554 5200 (information)

www.teacherline.org.uk

Trust for the Study of Adolescence (TSA)

A charity undertaking research, training and publications; seeks to influence policy makers. Concerned with increasing understanding about adolescence and young adulthood.

23 New Road, Brighton BN1 1WZ

 Tel: 01273 693 311

info@tsa.uk.com

UK Council for Psychotherapy

Seeks to promote the art and science of psychotherapy, and promote research and education in the field.

2nd Floor, Edward House, 2 Wakley Street, London EC1 7LT

☎ Tel: 020 7436 3002

 www.psychotherapy.org.uk
info@psychotherapy.org.uk

WHO (World Health Organisation)

UN specialised agency for health.
Avenue Appia 20, Geneva 27, Switzerland

☎ Tel: (+41 22)791 21 11

YoungMinds

Concerned directly with children and young people. Offers comprehensive website, information service, a magazine, and leaflets and booklets for young people, parents and professionals.

48–50 St John Street, London EC1M 4DG

☎ Tel: 020 7336 8445 (parents' information service: 0800 081 2138); Fax: 020 7336 8446

 www.youngminds.org.uk

Youth Access

National membership organisation for young people's information, advice, counselling and support services.

1–2 Taylors Yard, 67 Alderbrook Road, London SW12 8AD

☎ Tel: 020 8772 9900
admin@youthaccess.org.uk

Specific

ADHD (attention-deficit and hyperactivity disorder)

ADD Information Services (ADDISS)

Information and resources for parents, sufferers, teachers or health professionals.

10 Station Road, Mill Hill, London, NW7 2JU

☎ Tel: 020 8906 9068

 www.addiss.co.uk

Anxiety

Anxiety Care

East London charity helping people to recover from anxiety disorders and to maintain recovery.

Cardinal Heenan Centre, 326 High Road, Ilford, Essex 1G1 1QP
☎ Tel: 020 8262 8891; 135: 020 8478 3400
🖰 www.anxietycare.org.uk

National Phobic Society

A user-led organisation working to relieve those living with anxiety disorders.

Zion Community Resource Centre, 339 Stretton Road, Hulme, Manchester M15 4ZY
☎ Tel: 0870 122 2325
🖰 www.phobics-society.org.uk

No panic

Charity concerned with panic attacks, phobias, obsessive-compulsive disorder, generalised anxiety disorder and tranquilliser withdrawal.

93 Brands Farm Way, Telford, Shropshire TF3 2JQ
☎ Helpline: 0808 8080545
🖰 www.nopanic.org.uk

Social Anxiety Disorders Sufferers

🖰 www.social-anxiety.org

Autistic spectrum disorders

Autistic Society

🖰 www.autisticsociety.org/

National Autistic Society

Offers advice, information and support.
393 City Road, London EC1V 1NG
☎ Tel: 020 7833 2299
nas@nas.org.uk

Bereavement

Child Bereavement Network

Concerned with improving access to information, guidance and support services.

8 Wakely Street, London EC1V 7QE
☎ Tel: 020 7843 6309
🖰 www.ncb.org.uk/cbn

Cruse Bereavement Care

Provides counselling and support as well as information, advice, education and training.

Cruse House, 126 Sheen Road, Richmond, Surrey TW9 1UR
☎ Tel: 020 8939 9530; helpline: 0870 167 1677
🖱 www.crusebereavementcare.org.uk/

National Association of Bereavement Services

Provides information about services, training and referral.
2 Plough Yard, London EC2A
☎ Tel: 020 7247 1080

Winston's Wish

Offers practical support and guidance to families and professionals concerned about a grieving child.

Clara Burgess Centre, Bayshill Road, Cheltenham GL50 3AW
☎ Tel: 0845 2030 405
info@winstonswish.org.uk
🖱 www.winstonswish.org.uk/

Bullying

Anti-bullying Campaign

10 Borough High Street, London SE1 9QQ
☎ Tel: 020 7378 1446 (advice line)

Bullying Online

help@bullying.co.uk
🖱 www.bullying.co.uk/

Childwatch

19 Spring Bank, Hull, East Yorkshire HU3 1AF
☎ Tel: 01482 325 552
🖱 www.childwatch.org.uk

Kidscape

Charity established to prevent bullying and child abuse. Offers a helpline and a range of resources, and carries out research.

2 Grosvenor Gardens, London SW1W 0DH
☎ Tel: 08451 205 204
🖱 www.kidscape.org.uk/

Depression

Depression Alliance

Seeks to raise awareness of depression and provide information and support services.

PO Box 1022, 35 Westminster Bridge Road, London SE1 7JB

Tel: 0845 123 2320
www.depressionalliance.org/

Depressives Anonymous (Fellowship of)

A nationwide self-help organisation made up of members and groups who meet locally for mutual support.

Box FDA, Ormiston House, 32–36 Pelham Street, Nottingham NG1 2EG

Tel: 0870 774 4320
www.depressionanon.co.uk

Domestic violence

Victim Support

A charity helping people to cope with the effects of crime.

Local branch in the telephone directory

Women's Aid Domestic Violence Helpline

Tel: 0345 023 468

Eating disorders

Eating Disorders Association

Works to improve the quality of life for people affected by eating disorders. Provides information, help and support, and campaigns for improved standards and availability of treatment and care for sufferers.

103 Prince of Wales Road, Norwich NR1 1DW
Tel: 0870 770 3256; youth helpline: 0845 634 7650
info@edauk.com

Eating Disorders Research Unit

Institute of Psychiatry, King's College London, De Crespigny Park, London SE5 8AF
www.eatingresearch.com

Lucy Serpell's Eating Disorders Resources Page

 News, research, reports, conferences and opinions on eating disorders.
http://edr.org.uk

Mirror Mirror

 Website concerned with body image.
www.miror-mirror.org/eatdis.htm

Overeaters Anonymous

 A fellowship of individuals who are recovering from overeating.
www.oa.org

Emotional and Behavioural difficulties

SEBDA (Social, Emotional and Behavioural Difficulties Association)

Promotes excellence in services for children and young people with SEBD.

Church House, 1 St Andrew's View, Penrith, Cumbria CA107YF
 Tel: 01768 210 510
admin@sebda.org
www.sebda.co.uk

Enuresis

ERIC (Enuresis Resource and Information Centre)

Provides information for children, parents and professionals concerned about wetting and soiling.

34 Old School House, Britannia Road, Kingswood, Bristol BS15 8DB
 Tel: 0845 370 8008
www.eric.org.uk

Ethnic minority organisations

African-Caribbean Mental Health Association

Provides legal advice, housing support, counselling and psychotherapy to Afro-Caribbean people experiencing mental health problems.

Suites 34 and 37, 49 Effra Road, Brixton, London SW2 1BZ
 Tel: 020 7737 3603
www.directions-plus.org.uk

African-Caribbean Mental Health Service

Zion Community Health and Resource Centre, Hulme Clinic, Royce Road, Hulme, Manchester M15 5FQ

☎ Tel: 0161 226 9562

Asian Men's Group

Mandala Centre, Gregory Boulevard, Nottingham NG7 6LB

☎ Tel: 0115 960 6082

Black Mental Health Resource Centre

Bushberry House, 4 Laurel Mount, St Mary's Road, Leeds LS7 3JX

☎ Tel: 0113 237 4229

Chinese Mental Health Association

Provides direct services and raises awareness in the Chinese community and society generally.

Zenith House, 155 Curtain Road, London EC2A 3QY

☎ Tel: 020 7613 1008

🖱 www.cmha.org.uk

Jewish Association for the Mentally Ill

16a North End Road, London NW11 7PH

☎ Tel: 020 8458 2223; Fax: 020 8458 1117

🖱 www.mentalhealth-jami.org.uk

Qalb Centre

Counselling and complementary therapies for Asian, African and African-Caribbean people with emotional problems.

Low Hall Lane, Walthamstow, London E17 8BE

☎ Tel: 020 8521 5223

theqalbcentre@hotmail.com

Refugee Council

Largest organisation in the UK working with asylum seekers and refugees, to ensure that their needs and concerns are addressed.

240–250 Ferndale Road, London SW9 8BB

☎ Tel: 020 7346 6700

🖱 www.refugeecouncil.org.uk

Vishvas (Asian Women's Mental Health)

A culturally sensitive and accessible mental health service offering information, support and counselling for the South Asian community.

☎ Tel: 020 7928 9889

🖰 www.cio.org.uk

HIV/Aids

National AIDS Helpline

85/89 Duke Street, Liverpool L15 AP

☎ Tel: 0800 567 123

Terrence Higgins Trust

For people affected by HIV.

52–54 Grays Inn Road, London WC1 8JU

☎ Tel: 0845 1221 200

info@tht.org.uk

🖰 www.tht.org.uk

Manic depression

The Manic Depression Fellowship

Organisation offering membership and working to help people with bipolar disorder/manic depression take control of their lives.

Castle Works, 21 St George's Road, London SE1 6ES

☎ Tel: 08456 340540

🖰 www.mdf.org.uk

mdf@mdf.org.uk

Obsessive-compulsive disorder (OCD)

OCD Action

A registered charity providing information, advice and support to people with OCD.

Aberdeen Centre, 22-24 Highbury Grove, London N5 2EA

☎ Tel: 0870 360 6232; helpline: 0845 390 6232

🖰 www.ocdaction.org.uk/home.htm

OCD UK

Information and support for sufferers from OCD.

OCD-UK, PO Box 8115, Nottingham NG7 1YT
 Tel: 0870 126 9506
 http://www.ocduk.org

Phobia

Triumph over Phobia (TOP UK)

Helps sufferers of phobia or obsessive-compulsive disorder.

PO Box 3760, Bath BA2 4WY
 Tel: 0845 600 9601
www.triumphoverphobia.com

Schizophrenia

Rethink Severe Mental Illness (Formerly National Schizophrenia Fellowship)

28 Castle Street, Kingston-Upon Thames, Surrey KT1 1SS
www.rethink.org.uk

Schizophrenia.com

Provides in-depth information, support and education relating to schizophrenia.
www.schizophrenia.com

Seasonal affective disorder (SAD)

SAD Association

A voluntary organisation and charity which informs the public and health professions about SAD and supports and advises sufferers from the illness.

PO Box 989, Steyning, West Sussex BN44 3HG
 Tel: 01903 814942
www.sada.org.uk

Self-Harm

National Self-Harm Network

A survivor-led organisation that campaigns for the rights and understanding of people who self-harm, but whose priority is to support victims and survivors.

PO Box 7264, Nottingham NG1 6WJ

 www.nshn.co.uk/index2.html

info@nshn.co.uk

The Young People and Self-Harm Information Service

 www.ncb.org.uk/selfharm

Sexual relationships

Brook Advisory Centres

Free and confidential sexual health advice and contraception for young people up to the age of 25.

421 Highgate Studios, 53–79 Highgate Road, London NW5 1TL

 Tel: 020 7284 6040

www.brook.org.uk

Family Planning Association

Seeks to improve sexual health. Provides information, training and publications.

2–12 Pentonville Road, London N1 9FP

 Tel: 08455 310 1334

www.fpa.org.uk

Special educational needs

National Association for Special Educational Needs (NASEN)

Leading organisation to promote the education, training, and advancement and development of all those with special and additional support needs. Membership available. NASEN produces a number of journals and publications.

NASEN House, 4–5 Amber Business Village, Amber Close, Amington, Tamworth B77 4RP

 www.nasen.org.uk

British Dyslexia Association

98 London Road, Reading, Berks R61 5AU

Tel: 01734 662 677; helpline: 01734 668 271

Stress

International Stress Management Association

Promotes sound knowledge and best practice in the prevention and reduction of human stress.

PO Box 26, South Petherton TA13 5WY

 Tel: 07000 780 430

www.isma.org.uk/index.htm

Substance abuse

Alcoholics Anonymous

Helps people who drink alcohol excessively to change their lives.

 Tel: 0845 769 7555

www.alcoholics-anonymous.org.uk

aanewcomer@runbox.com

Alcohol Concern

Acts as a national umbrella body tackling alcohol-related harm.

Waterbridge House, 32-36 Loman Street, London SE1 0EE

 Tel: 020 7928 7377

www.alcoholconcern.org.uk/

contact@alcoholconcern.org.uk

National Drugs Helpline

 Tel: 0800 77 66 00 (24-hour helpline)

www.ndh.org.uk

Talk to Frank

Information and advice on drug misuse.

Tel: 0800 776 600

www.talktofrank.com/

frank@talktofrank.com

Turning Point

A leading social care organisation providing services for people with complex needs, including those with mental health and drug and alcohol misuse.

New Loom House, 101 Backchurch Lane, London E1 1LU

 Tel: 020 7702 2300

www.turning-point.co.uk/

info@turning-point.co.uk

Young carers

Young carers

20–25 Glasshouse Yard, London EC1A 4JS
☎ Tel: 020 7490 8898

Useful websites

BBC Mental Health

🖱 www.bbc.co.uk/health/mental

The Collaborative for Academic, Social, and Emotional Learning (CASEL)

Concerned with the relationship between social emotional skills and learning.
🖱 www.casel.org

E-mental-health.com

🖱 www.emental-com

Incentive Plus

Company that provides a catalogue of resources in the areas of emotional competence, emotional health and positive behaviour in children and young people.

☎ Tel: 01908 5261 120

Internet Mental Health

🖱 www.mentalhealth.com

LDA

Publishes useful resources catalogue.

Abbeygate House, East Road, Cambridge CB1 1DB

☎ Tel: 0845 120 4776

Mental Health for Teens

Useful Australian website.

🖱 www.mydr.com.au

National Mental Health Information Centre

Useful US website.

 www.mentalhealth.samhsa.gov

Psychiatry24x7

Information on mental illness.

www.psywww.com/

www.readthesigns.org

Information on a range of mental illnesses.

Teenage Health Freak

Information for teenagers.

www.teenagehealthfreak.org

The Site

www.thesite.org/

UCLA School Mental Health Project

Useful website for anyone interested in school-based mental health.

http://psych.ucla.edu/temphome.

References

American Academy of Child and Adolescent Psychiatry. (2003) Children of parents with mental illness, *Journal of the American Academy of Child and Adolescent Psychiatry*, 39.

Antidote (2003) *The emotional literacy handbook*. London: David Fulton.

Antonovsky, A (1987) *Unravelling the mysteries of health: how people manage stress and stay well*. San Francisco, CA: Jossey-Bass.

Atkinson, M and Hornby, G (2002) *Mental health handbook for schools*. New York: RoutledgeFalmer.

Audit Commission (1999) *Children in mind: Child and Adolescent Mental Health Services (CAMHS)*. Briefing, September 1999.

Ayalon, O and Flasher, A (1993) *Chain reaction: children and divorce*. London: Jessica Kingsley.

BACP (2001) *Good practice guidance for counselling in schools*. Rugby: British Association for Counselling and Psychotherapy.

BACP (2002) *Ethical framework for good practice in counselling and psychotherapy*. Rugby: British Association for Counselling and Psychotherapy.

BACP (2005) *Counselling and psychotherapy resources directory*. Rugby: British Association for Counselling and Psychotherapy.

BBC News (2001) Too stressed to go to school. 19 June 2001.

Bunting, M (2004) Today's youth: anxious, depressed, anti-social, *Guardian*, 13 September 2004.

Carey, B (2005) Separating troubles from illness. *New York Times*, Thursday 16 June 2005.

ChildLine (2002) *Setting up a peer support scheme*. London: ChildLine.

ChildLine. (2004) *Can I talk to you again? Restoring the emotional and mental well-being of children and young people*. London: ChildLine.

Comer, R (2001) *Abnormal psychology*. New York: Worth.

Cooper, P and Bilton, K (2002) *Attention deficit/hyperactivity disorder: a practical guide for teachers*. London: David Fulton.

Cowie, H and Wallace, P (2000) *Peer Support in Action*. London: Sage.

Cowie, H, Boardman, C, Dawkins, J and Jennifer, D (2004) *Emotional health and well-being*. London: Paul Chapman Publishing.

Csóti, M (2003) *School phobia, panic attacks and anxiety in children*. London: Jessica Kingsley.

Cumine, V, Leach, J and Stevenson, G (2000) *Asperger syndrome: a practical guide for teachers*. London: David Fulton.

Department for Education and Skills (2001) *Promoting children's mental health within early years and school settings*. London: DfES.

Department for Education and Skills (2004) *Every child matters*. London: DfES.

Dogra, N, Parkin, A, Gale, F and Frake, C (2002) *A multidisciplinary handbook of child and adolescent mental health for front-line professionals*. London: Jessica Kingsley.

Donnellan, C (ed.) (2000) *Issues 51: self-harm and suicide*. Cambridge: Independence.

Dowling, M (2000) *Young children's personal, social and emotional development*. London: Paul Chapman Publishing.

Draucker, C B (1992) *Counselling survivors of childhood sexual abuse*. London: Sage.

Dwivedi, K N and Harper, P B (2004) *Promoting the emotional well-being of children and adolescents and preventing their emotional ill health: a handbook*. London: Jessica Kingsley.

Educational Resources Information Centre (1995) *Fostering resilience in children*. ERIC/EECE Publications.

Faber, A and Mazlish, E (1980) *How to talk so kids will listen and listen so kids will talk*. New York: Avon.

Fogell, J and Long, R (1999) *Supporting pupils with emotional difficulties*. London: David Fulton.

Gilbert, S (2000) *Counselling for eating disorders*. London: Sage.

Gottman, J (1997) *The heart of parenting: how to raise an emotionally intelligent child*. London: Bloomsbury.

Gray, G (1997) *Talking about it: promoting mental health in schools*. An educational resource. Meridian Broadcasting Charitable Trust.

Gross, R and McIlveen, R (1996) *Abnormal psychology*. London: Hodder and Stoughton.

Hallam, R (1992) *Counselling for anxiety problems*. London: Sage.

Harley-Brewer, E (2001) *Learning to trust and trusting to learn: how schools can affect children's mental health*. London: Institute for Public Policy Research.

Harris, P (1989) *Children and emotion*. London: Blackwell.

Health Development Agency (2004) *Promoting emotional health and well-being through the national healthy school standard*. London: Department of Health/Department for Education and Skills.

Hill, K (1995) *The long sleep: young people and suicide*. London: Virago.

Hipp, E (1995) *Help for the hard times: getting through loss*. New York: Hazelden.

Indiana University Center for Adolescent Studies (1996) Holly: a student's story of hope. *Teacher Talk*, 3 (2).

Klein, R (2000) *Defying disaffection: how schools are winning the hearts and minds of reluctant students*. Stoke-on-Trent: Trentham Books.

Lewis, C, Johnson, A and Lewis, N (1994) *Eating disorders: guidance for teachers*. Biggin Hill Family Reading Centre.

Lindsay, B and Elsegood, J (eds) (1996) *Working with children in grief and loss*. London: Baillière Tindall.

McNamara, S (2000) *Stress in young people: what's new and what can we do?* London: Continuum.

McNamara, S (2001) *Stress management programme for secondary school students*. New York: Routledge Falmer.

Mental Health Foundation (1999) *Bright futures: promoting children and young people's mental health*. London: Mental Health Foundation.

Mental Health Foundation (2002a) *The mental health of looked-after children. Bright futures: working with vulnerable young people*. London: Mental Health Foundation.

Mental Health Foundation (2002b) *The mental health needs of young people with emotional and behavioural difficulties. Bright futures: working with vulnerable young people*. London: Mental Health Foundation.

Mental Health Foundation (2002c) *The mental health of young offenders. Bright futures: working with vulnerable young people*. London: Mental Health Foundation.

Mental Health Foundation (2002d) *Peer support report: executive summary*. London: Mental Health Foundation.

Mental Health Foundation (2002e) *The promoting engagement project*. Updates Vol. 3, Issue 16. Mental Health Foundation. Available free online at www.mentalhealth.org.uk/page.cfm?page-code=PBUP03

Mind (2001) *Children, young people and mental health*. Fact sheet. London: Mind.

National Children's Bureau. Peer Support Forum Briefing Papers. Available online at www.ncb.org.uk/psf/publications.asp?dept=26.

NHS National Health Advisory Service (1995) *Together we stand. The commissioning role and management of child and adolescent mental health services*. London: HMSO.

NSPCC (2002) *Mentally ill parents and children's welfare. Information Briefing*. London: NSPCC.

Office for National Statistics (2000) *Mental health of children and adolescents in Great Britain*. London: Stationery Office.

Office for National Statistics (2003) *The mental health of young people looked after by local authorities.* London: Stationery Office.

Ofsted (2005) *Healthy minds: promoting emotional health and well-being in schools.* Available free online at www.ofsted.gov.uk

Persaud, R (2001) *Staying sane: how to make your mind work for you.* New York: Bantam.

Pilgrim, D (2005) *Key concepts in mental health.* London: Sage.

Pinfold, V (2003) Awareness in action: changing discriminatory and negative attitudes to mental health should start at school. *Mental Health Today*, July/August.

Prever, M (2004) *Exploring mental health: a teaching resource for schools – for work with students aged 14 to 16.* Rugby: British Association for Counselling and Psychotherapy.

Rogers, C R (1951) *On becoming a person.* Boston: Houghton Mifflin.

Rosenhan, D and Seligman, M (1989) *Abnormal psychology.* New York: Norton.

Royal College of Psychiatrists (1999a) *Mental health and growing up.* 2nd edn. *Divorce or separation of parents – the impact on children and adolescents. Fact sheet 15 for parents and teachers.* Available free online at www.rcpsych.ac.uk/info/mhgu/index.htm.

Royal College of Psychiatrists (1999b) *Mental health and growing up.* 2nd edn. *Domestic violence – its effects on children. Factsheet 18 for parents and teachers.* Available free online at www.rcpsych.ac.uk/info/mhgu/index.htm

Royal College of Psychiatrists (1999c) *Mental health and growing up.* 2nd edn. *The emotional cost of bullying. Fact sheet 19 for parents and teachers.* Available free online at www.rcpsych.ac.uk/info/mhgu/index.htm.

Royal College of Psychiatrists (2002a) *Mental health and growing up.* 2nd edn. *Behaviour problems and conduct disorder. Factsheet 4 for parents and teachers.* Available free online at www.rcpsych.ac.uk/info/mhgu/index.htm.

Royal College of Psychiatrists (2002b) *Mental health and growing up.* 2nd edn. *Death in the family – helping children to cope. Factsheet 16 for parents and teachers.* Available free online at www.rcpsych.ac.uk/info/mhgu/index.htm

Royal College of Psychiatrists (2002c) *Mental health and growing up.* 2nd edn. *Deliberate self-harm in young people. Factsheet 30 for teachers and parents.* Available free online at www.rcpsych.ac.uk/info/mhgu/index.htm

Royal College of Psychiatrists (2002d) *Mental health and growing up.* 2nd edn. *Depression in children and young people. Fact sheet 25 for parents and teachers.* www.rcpsych.ac.uk/info/mhgu/index.htm.

Royal College of Psychiatrists (2003) Workshops help young people challenge the stigma of mental illness. Press Release, 1 April 2003.

Salzberger-Wittenberg, I, Williams, G and Osborne, E (1983) *The emotional experience of learning and teaching.* London: Karnac.

The Samaritans (1997) *Youth pack. Helping you help young people.* London: The Samaritans.

Sanderson, C (1995) *Counselling adult survivors of child sexual abuse.* 2nd edn. London: Jessica Kingsley.

Smith, C and McKee, S (2005) *Becoming an emotionally healthy school.* London: Paul Chapman Publishing.

Smith, E (2004) Britain: teenagers driven to depression and suicide by exam pressures. Published online by the International Committee of the Fourth International at www.wsws.org/articles/testdir/jun2004/dep-j25.shtml.

Social Exclusion Unit (2003) *Mental health and social exclusion.* London: Office of the Deputy Prime Minister.

Strong, M (2000) *A bright red scream. Self-mutilation and the language of pain.* London: Virago.

Surgeon General (2000) *Report on the Surgeon General's conference on children's mental health: a national action agenda.* Washington, DC: Department of Health and Human Services.

Swan-Jackson, A (1997) *Caught in the middle: teenagers talk about their parents' divorce.* London: Piccadilly.

Times Educational Supplement (2003) The issue: parents at war. 24 October 2003; www.tes.co.uk/search/story/?story_id=385717.

Times Educational Supplement (2004a) The issue: children in care. 18 June 2004; www.tes.co.uk/search/story/?story_id=396497.

Times Educational Supplement (2004b) The issue: children's mental health, 10 September 2004 www.tes.co.uk/search/story/?story_id=399543

Times Educational Supplement (2005) The issue: self-harm. 18 March.

Titterton, M, Hill, M and Smart, H (2002) Mental health promotion and the early years: the evidence base: risk, protection and resilience. *Journal of Mental Health Promotion*, 1(1).

Tones, K (1981) Health education: prevention or subversion? *Royal Society of Health Journal*, 101: 114–17.

Tormey, N (2005) *Every school should have one: how peer support schemes make schools better*. London: ChildLine.

UCLA (1996) Addressing barriers to learning. Mental health in schools: emerging trends. *Newsletter*, University of California, Los Angeles School Mental Health Project. 1(1), Winter.

Vellacott, J (2005) Something inside us, *YoungMinds Magazine*, 77: 18.

Weare, K (1999) *Promoting mental, emotional and social health: a whole school approach*. London: Routledge.

Weare, K (2003) *Developing the emotionally literate school*. London: Paul Chapman Publishing.

Williams, M (1997) *Cry of Pain. Understanding suicide and self-harm*. London: Penguin.

Wilson, P (2003) *Young minds in our schools: a guide for teachers and others working in schools*. London: YoungMinds.

Winfield, L (1994) *Developing resilience in urban youth*. University of Southern California Graduate School of Education, NCREL Monograph.

World Federation for Mental Health (2003) *World mental health day: emotional and behavioural disorders of children and adolescents*. Baltimore, MD: WFMH.

World Health Organisation (2001) *Strengthening mental health promotion*. Fact sheet no. 220. Geneva: WHO.

YoungMinds (1996) *Mental health in your school: a guide for teachers and others working in schools*. London: Jessica Kingsley.

YoungMinds Policy for mental health services for adolescents and young adults. Available online at www.youngminds.org.uk/adolescentpolicy.

INDEX